The Curtain

Witness and Memory in Wartime Holland

Life Writing Series

In the **Life Writing Series,** Wilfrid Laurier University Press publishes life writing and new life-writing criticism in order to promote autobiographical accounts, diaries, letters, and testimonials written and/or told by women and men whose political, literary, or philosophical purposes are central to their lives. **Life Writing** features the accounts of ordinary people, written in English, or translated into English from French or the languages of the First Nations or from any of the languages of immigration to Canada. **Life Writing** will also publish original theoretical investigations about life writing, as long as they are not limited to one author or text.

Priority is given to manuscripts that provide access to those voices that have not traditionally had access to the publication process.

Manuscripts of social, cultural, and historical interest that are considered for the series, but are not published, are maintained in the **Life Writing Archive** of Wilfrid Laurier University Library.

Series Editor
Marlene Kadar
Humanities Division, York University

Manuscripts to be sent to
Brian Henderson, Director
Wilfrid Laurier University Press
75 University Avenue West
Waterloo, Ontario, Canada N2L 3C5

HENRY G. SCHOGT

The Curtain

Witness and Memory in Wartime Holland

Wilfrid Laurier University Press

We acknowledge the support of the Canada Council for the Arts for our publishing program. We acknowledge the financial support of the Government of Canada through the Book Publishing Industry Development Program for our publishing activities.

National Library of Canada Cataloguing in Publication

Henry, Schogt G., 1927-
    The curtain : witness and memory in wartime Holland / Henry G. Schogt.

(Life writing series)
ISBN 978-0-88920-396-9 (pbk).—ISBN 978-0-88920-618-2 (PDF).—ISBN 978-1-55458-781-0 (epub)

    1. World War, 1939-1945—Netherlands. 2. World War, 1939-1945—Personal narratives, Dutch. 3. Schogt, Henry G., 1927- . 4. Schogt family. 5. World War, 1939-1945—Jews—Netherlands. 6. Frenkel family. 7. Netherlands—History— German occupation, 1940-1945. I. Title. II. Series.

DJ283.S35A3 2003   940.54'81492   C2003-901963-2

© 2003 Wilfrid Laurier University Press
Waterloo, Ontario, Canada N2L 3C5
www.wlupress.wlu.ca

Cover and text design by William Rueter.

About the cover
The Dutch artist Hendrik Nicolaas Werkman (1882-1945) lived in Groningen. He was involved with the Resistance, was apprehended in March 1945, and executed 10 April 1945 by the SD, three days before Groningen was liberated. During the German occupation, Werkman, out of sympathy with the Jews, made two series of ten prints for Chassidic stories, as retold by Martin Buber (1878-1965). One of these, *The Angel of the Last Consolation*, was chosen for the cover of this book.

    I am grateful to the Groningen Museum for the permission to reproduce Werkman's work, and to Will Rueter, who designed the cover and the layout and whose invaluable friendship and support are very precious to me.—H.G.S.

No part of this publication may be reproduced, stored in a retrieval system or transmitted, in any form or by any means, without the prior written consent of the publisher or a licence from The Canadian Copyright Licensing Agency (Access Copyright). For an Access Copyright licence, visit www.accesscopyright.ca or call toll free to 1-800-893-5777.

To the memory of my parents

Ida Jacoba van Rijn (1891-1972)
and
Johannes Herman Schogt (1892-1958)

and my parents-in-law

Betsy Adèle Wiener (1898-1944)
and
Salomon Philip Frenkel (1889-1944)

Contents

Prologue	ix
Acknowledgements	xi
Introduction	1
Remembering Alex, 1939-43	11
The Fortune Teller, 1936-43	29
Mr. Rozenberg's Cigars, 1932-45	43
In the Dark, 1940-55	67
Mussels, 1936-42	81
Lilies of the Valley and Asparagus, 1942-45	99
The Curtain, 1942-44	113
Appendix	125

The Netherlands, 1940-45.

Prologue

In the winter of 1954, we went on a skating trip north of Amsterdam with a group of friends, all of whom were, like us, in their mid-twenties. Between the village of Jisp and the town of Purmerend, Corrie and I singled each other out from among the group. We skated the last stretch against the wind in the traditional Dutch way, I with my hands behind my back, Corrie holding on to me. Although we belonged to the same circle of students and had many friends in common, we had only met briefly once or twice, and did not know each other before this trip. Corrie was in her final years of an English degree, similar to a Canadian M.A. I, having completed an equivalent program in French and Russian, had become a travelling salesman in languages. I taught French part-time at the University of Utrecht, Russian at the University of Groningen once a week, and French at the Montessori Lyceum in The Hague. Yet Amsterdam remained the centre of my universe, and when we married in the spring of 1955 we settled there without considering other options. It was ten years after the end of World War II, and the general mood was optimistic in spite of the Cold War. Reconstruction of our devastated country was well underway. Moderate socialism had reduced pre-war inequalities, and concerns about the depletion of raw materials and the extinction of many species of plants and animals had not yet spread. The first years of our marriage were in harmony with the times. We knew that life had not been easy for either of us, but we hardly talked about our experiences during the war years. We looked forward to a future with children. I was even, albeit reluctantly, starting work on a doctoral thesis, and there was no time for dwelling on the past.

Later we realized, however, that the five years from 1940 to 1945 could neither be suppressed nor forgotten, and that what had happened in that relatively short period had a lasting influence on our outlook on life. It coloured our contacts with friends and strangers, as well as our relations with our children. It is for this reason that we would like to share our memories of these crucial years. Canada, as became abundantly clear during the celebrations in 1995—the fiftieth anniversary of the liberation of the Netherlands by Canadian troops—has strong emotional ties with the Dutch people. Yet apart from the liberation itself, the enthusiastic reception of the Canadians by the Dutch, and the desolate state of the Netherlands at that moment, little is known in Canada of what happened there during the war.

A short survey of the war years in Holland will make it easier to place some of the events described in these memoirs in their historical context. In the Appendix at the end of the book, a chronology of the measures taken by the Germans against the Jews living in the Netherlands gives an idea how methodically the Germans went about their self-imposed task of exterminating the Jews.

Of the seven episodes highlighting memorable events that took place in the war years, four are written in the first person and deal with my own memories, while three are based on what I was told by my wife and her relatives. The last of these three episodes deals with the fate of my parents-in-law, whom I never knew, to my deep sorrow. "Remembering Alex" was written in Dutch in 1987, and published in *De Gids*, a Dutch literary journal, in 1988. Over the next ten years I completed this small collection of memoirs with Canadian, rather than Dutch, readers in mind.

I have noted the crucial years of each episode to help readers find their way through the network of intersecting stories in which the protagonists of one section may reappear in the background of another one. Taken together, our stories may give some idea of how Dutch people lived, and of the sorrow and suffering inflicted by the Germans on innocent people. Yet it will always remain impossible to understand how it could have happened.

Acknowledgements

I would like to thank Jean Smith and Susan Sourial for their graciously offered help in typing the manuscript, and Ed Burstynsky for reading the text and putting it on a disk, and for his continuous encouragement.

I am greatly indebted to Ian Montagnes and Ben Shek who both read the manuscript, corrected mistakes, and eliminated many of the traces of my Dutch origin.

Paul Socken was instrumental in getting me in touch with Wilfrid Laurier University Press. Without him, and without the friendly, efficient, accommodating help given by Carroll Klein, Heather Blain-Yanke, and Leslie Macredie, this book would never have been published.

Introduction

IN THE BEGINNING, when the country was not taking part in the war, the Dutch had a misplaced sense of security; again, as in World War I, they were neutral, and if the unthinkable happened and the Germans declared war, the Dutch army would be prepared. In September 1939 the military even requisitioned horses, and the Waterlinie (Water defence line) was ready. It could be flooded at any moment when necessary for the protection of the western part of the country with its big cities: Amsterdam, Rotterdam, The Hague, and Utrecht. Pessimists objected that the country was too small and the German air force too fast for the Dutch to protect their cities, all less than two hundred kilometres away from the German border.

Meanwhile, in the "phony war," the British soldiers were singing: "We are hanging out our washing on the Siegfried line," the French were sitting behind the fortifications of the Maginot line, and the Germans were doing nothing, or so it seemed.

It was a rude awakening when they invaded Denmark and Norway, but even then many people believed that it would not happen in Holland. My parents, who had studied Scandinavian languages in their spare time, and were in correspondence with Danish and Norwegian acquaintances, were almost convinced that the Netherlands would be next. Their fears were not ungrounded: on the night of 10 May 1940, the Germans started their attack. The Dutch army was outnumbered and overrun by the better-equipped enemy. The Water defence line did not stop the German air force, which not only bombed Dutch fortifications but also dropped thousands of parachutists behind the front lines. When German bombers destroyed the centre of Rotterdam, the hopelessness of the situation became clear, and the next day, 15 May 1940, the five-day war ended and the five-year-long occupation began.

The country was in shock and tried to reassure itself that the occupying Germans acted correctly. If one did not look too closely it was easy to hold on to that illusion: life continued almost unchanged the first few months. Unlike Belgium, where the *Wehrmacht* (German army) was the highest authority, the Netherlands kept their civil administration under SS auspices. The SS (short for *Schutzstaffel* [protective squadron], Hitler's bodyguard, and later the elite guard of the Nazi militia, deployed to suppress opposition in Germany and conquered countries) turned out to be much harsher than the army. At first, however, the term "civil administration" suggested the opposite to the Dutch. The Germans arrested a few political enemies, but that was to be expected in a war. The first restrictive measures against the Jews seemed petty and of little consequence to outsiders. The Resistance movement was only starting and was uncoordinated. Small groups operated in isolation without much experience of underground, subversive activities. Only the communists were not neophytes in this area, but they found themselves in an awkward position after Von Ribbentrop and Molotov had signed a treaty making Germany and the Soviet Union allies, if not friends. When the invasion of the Soviet Union by the Germans put an end to the alliance in June 1941, most Dutch communists had already abandoned any pretense of approving the treaty between the admired Russians and the Germans whom they detested.

In the thirteen months between the surrender of the Dutch in May 1940 and the moment the Germans crossed into Soviet territory, the grip of the occupying forces on all aspects of life in the Netherlands had tightened a great deal. Rationing had been introduced, the press was no longer free, and all levels of government were under German control. The reaction from the Dutch who were directly involved in the measures was one of compliance under protest, most of the time muttered sotto voce, but on a few occasions spoken out loudly.

When, less than six months after overpowering the country, the Germans required a declaration from everybody working in the public sector, including teaching and support staff in schools and universities, stating that they belonged (or did not belong) to the Aryan (i.e.,

Caucasian) race, almost everybody signed in what came close to complete silence. However, three weeks later, when all Jews were dismissed from teaching and administrative positions in all institutions of learning and education, some university students and faculty staged protests, and classes in the institutions involved were suspended. In February of the following year (1941) the only major public protest, later known as the February strike, was staged. Dutch Nazi police had started openly to attack Jews and Jewish businesses in the centre of Amsterdam. In the resulting street fights a policeman died. The Germans sealed off the Jewish quarter, and at the same time a Jewish Council (*Joodse Raad*) was created, after the Eastern European model, to take responsibility for Jewish affairs. The situation in the inner city remained tense, and on the February 22 and 23 the Germans rounded up more than four hundred men as hostages and sent them to Mauthausen, a concentration camp with a notoriously cruel regime.

Two days later, on February 25, the longshoremen went on a solidarity strike to protest the way in which the Germans treated the Jews. From the harbour the protest spread to the city. Public transport stopped and many shops closed. A few towns in the vicinity of Amsterdam joined, while the rest of the country watched from the sidelines. The strike, which lasted only two days, was a boost for Dutch morale, but did not stop or even slow down the German plans. In the Netherlands, as everywhere in Western Europe, the Germans intended to rid countries of Jews in a series of planned stages, whereas the destruction of Eastern European Jewry was in many cases immediate. In *Persecution, Extermination, Literature* Sem Dresden writes: "What Jews had to endure in the twelve years that national socialism was in force has been described time and again. From numerous studies, it appears that after the conquest of Poland, Western Europe, and a part of Russia, the order and tempo of the events in store for them differed from one region to another, although the final end was the same for all."[1]

In the first two years of the occupation the Resistance was mainly concerned with aiding political fugitives, acts of sabotage, and estab-

---

[1] Sem Dresden, *Persecution, Extermination, Literature*, trans. Henry G. Schogt (Toronto: University of Toronto Press, 1995), 63; originally published as *Vervolging, Vernietiging, Literatuur* (Amsterdam: Meulenhoff, 1991).

lishing contact with England and with the Dutch government in exile in London. When in the summer of 1942 the full-scale deportation of Dutch Jews to the extermination camps in Poland began, the Resistance movement was ill-prepared to provide safe shelter and food for so many people. By the time the underground workers were better equipped to cope with the situation, many of their Jewish countrymen and their families had already been "resettled for work in the East," a phrase the Germans used to hide the fate that awaited their victims.

Jews who lived in small towns and villages had been ordered to move to Amsterdam, where they had to rely on the Jewish Council for help. When the deportations started and summonses were sent out to Jews to present themselves for work in the East, the Jewish Council played a key role in making the lists: first went those whose presence in Amsterdam was not essential to the community, or to the functioning of the German war machine. The Council's advice was to obey orders and to proceed to the collecting points indicated in the summonses.

When many ignored the summonses in spite of the Council's advice, the Germans and their Dutch helpers organized house raids, first at night, later also in the daytime. They sealed off streets and took their victims, sometimes with their luggage ready and waiting to be arrested, to a theatre called the Hollandse Schouwburg, which had been transformed into a temporary detention centre. Streetcars transported them to the Central Station, and from there trains to the transit camp, Westerbork. It was located in the northeast of the country, close to the German border, far, by Dutch standards, from Amsterdam.

The hunters also organized random street raids, picked up anybody wearing a yellow star, and took them to the German headquarters where the "Jewish resettlement" was organized. There they had to wait for many hours to have their papers checked and their fate decided. Jacques Presser describes his personal experiences in the inner courtyard of those headquarters in *Ashes in the Wind*:

> Aus der Fünten (Aus der Fünten, Ferdinand Hugo: Befehlshaber der Sicherheitspolizei und des SD—Zentralstelle für jüdische Auswanderung [Head of the Security Police and Security Service—Head Office for Jewish Resettlement]) had complained (bitterly) about

the distasteful job he had to do: "Why don't those who want it done, do it themselves?"

Because there is little reason to doubt Aus der Fünten's sincerity it seems doubly strange to see how he set to work on the next day. Here the writer [Jacques Presser] can rely almost completely on his own memory…he was one of the 2,000 picked up on August 6 and who spent the night with them in the open yard of the Zentralstelle. Throughout the next day, they had ample opportunity to watch Aus der Fünten at work—had he been a sadist he could have done no worse. He acted precisely like the German SS officer whom John Hersey has described in his novel *The Wall*, dividing the victims to left and right, to death and respite. Yes, on that August 7, 1942, the writer was able to watch him from early morning until five that evening, with long intervals during which the prisoners were consumed with unbearable anxiety. When Aus der Fünten first appeared on the steps, he was smoking one cigarette after another, and leaned nonchalantly against the wall. He was accompanied by a number of officials of the Jewish Council, including Leo de Wolff. Speaking very softly, he said as he looked across the courtyard: "There's too much noise here," and you could have heard a pin drop. Then he set to work. He had people placed in rows, usually no more than fifteen to twenty at a time, had them file before him, looked at them, inspected their papers, asked a few questions of De Wolff and then decided, without a single word, simply by waving his hand to the right or to the left.[2]

On that day, Presser writes, about six hundred people had not been checked when Aus der Fünten stopped his work at five o'clock. Together with those selected for work in the East, they were taken to the Hollandse Schouwburg, from where it was extremely difficult to get released, even with a *Sperre*.

One of the most effective means to create division and confusion within the Jewish community was the *Sperre*, the temporary exemption

---

2 Jacques Presser, *Ashes in the Wind: The Destruction of the Dutch Jews*, trans. by Arnold Pomerans (Toronto: Ryerson Press, 1968), 153; originally published as *Ondergang, de vervolging en verdelging van het Nederlandse Jodendom 1940-45* (The Hague: Nijhoff, 1965).

from work in the East. Dutch does not have an equivalent term for it, and in the years when the notion was important, they simply used *sper* or *sperre*, forms that the major Dutch dictionary still lists, with the comment, "used during the German occupation." Eventually these temporary exemptions proved to be temporary indeed, for not one of them remained valid until the end of the war.

Those who chose the risky solution of going into hiding put their fates in other people's hands. Some were lucky and could lead an almost but never completely normal life; others had to hide in places without any comfort, deprived of contact with the outside world. All depended more or less on the help of contact persons who secured the link between
the fugitive (and his hosts) and the underground organizations that provided help in the form of food, ration coupons, and false identity papers. In case of an arrest, it was crucial that the fugitives knew as little as possible about the source of the assistance they received. In spite of the efforts of the Resistance, and thanks to the cooperation or non-interference of Dutch civil servants, policemen, and public transport employees, the Germans succeeded in reaching the quota set in Berlin for the trains to Poland, and almost succeeded in completely annihilating Jewish life in the Netherlands.

In Amsterdam it was difficult not to be aware of what was happening to the Jews, but in many parts of the country people knew only that their Jewish fellow citizens had been forced to move to Amsterdam. Events at the eastern front and in Africa—where by 1943 the tide was turning against the invincible Germans—were followed much more closely than the plight of the Jews. Food rationing and ever-dwindling supplies of what was not rationed were daily concerns. Simply getting to work without a car (or a bicycle, the most common form of transportation, and one for which new tires were mostly unavailable) preoccupied many Dutch. Public transportation as well was drastically reduced. Eventually this lack of mobility became a major source of irritation. Everybody had to fend for him or herself. Although after the war a picture was created of a heroic people standing firm against the mighty enemy, in reality there was more petty egoism than heroic altruism during those years when the mettle of the Dutch was tested.

Introduction

The mood in the Netherlands finally changed with the collapse of the Eastern front as the Russians approached closer and closer to German territory, and with the Allied landing in the North, which dramatically changed the situation in the West. More people joined the Resistance, and many fence-sitters jumped to the winning side. For the Jews in hiding, apart from a renewed hope of survival, nothing had changed. The Germans continued their relentless search for Jewish fugitives; from Westerbork, the Tuesday trains continued to carry their loads to the extermination camps.

Towards the end of August 1944, it looked as if the definitive defeat of the Germans in the Netherlands was a matter of days. The Canadians and their allies were rapidly pushing through Belgium towards the Dutch border. The summer of great expectations reached its climax on Tuesday, 5 September, later referred to as Mad Tuesday. People were telling each other about miraculous advances in the south of the country, and rumours of Allied soldiers spotted in towns north of the rivers were readily accepted as eyewitness reports. Dutch Nazis, afraid of reprisals, were fleeing in droves to Germany, and even the Germans were in disarray. In the Amersfoort concentration camp there was no longer a clear authority, and some inmates managed to walk away to freedom. Those were heady times—the Dutch railway workers, who had for years worked for an institution that collaborated with the Germans, went on strike, and the liberators could be expected any moment.

But the Allied forces did not break through the German lines, and after fierce battles at the river Rhine near Arnhem, the front stabilized. The Germans held on to their positions north of the rivers Maas, Rhine, and Waal; the Canadians and their allies captured the territory south of them. In the part of the country still under German rule, people were bitterly disappointed. They had to cope with the punitive measures taken by the occupying authorities after the railway strike had begun and the railroad workers had gone into hiding. Although transport of food by boat from the farming regions in the east and north to the big cities in the west was far more important than that by rail, hardly any supplies reached the cities in the fall and the winter of 1944-45. The Germans deliberately created a famine by not letting any barges through. Electricity and gas were cut off; heating oil and coal were not available. Official rations provided five-hundred calories per day, but it was far from certain that all coupons could be honoured. Sugar beets and tulip bulbs became staples. Thousands of city dwellers died of starvation during the Famine Winter. For those in hiding who depended completely on outside help and could not go on expeditions into the countryside to barter valuables for food, the situation was especially difficult. Quite a few ventured outside their hiding places in spite of the danger. The Germans remained as vigilant as ever to catch Jews in this bleak winter.

The eastern part of the country and the northern provinces were liberated in April 1945, when the Canadians opened an offensive north of the rivers. The western, most densely populated provinces had to wait until the German forces surrendered unconditionally on 5 May 1945, five years minus five days after they had declared war on the Netherlands.

The following seven episodes recounting some of our experiences during the German occupation have been written to preserve the memories of those five crucial years. After fifty years these memories are still vivid, even though some contours tend to get blurred, while a few events stand out and seem to acquire more importance than when they took place. Looking back, one notices that one's good fortune depended on trivialities, and that bad luck could be equally fortuitous. Two twelve-year-old boys, playing soccer in the street, cunningly alerting the people who would otherwise have fallen into a trap set by a waiting policeman; a cleaning lady, who probably did not mean any harm, denounced the people at whose house she had worked two years earlier; a Nazi aunt who didn't denounce anybody, but with whom relations were to remain ambivalent at best—all played a role in my life during the conflict that overshadowed all other conflicts: the persecution and destruction of many of our Jewish friends and acquaintances by the Germans.

Dutch gentiles were free to participate in the Resistance against the policies of the occupying forces; they could also choose to stay on the sidelines, or even become active helpers of the persecutors. The overwhelming majority of the population opted for non-involvement, whereas members of the Resistance movement and Dutch Nazis formed small minorities. The three groups were not sharply separated from one another, however, and there were many grey zones of transition between them.

Although the common experiences of the war years immediately created a close bond when Corrie and I became acquainted, there are great differences between the situation in which my wife's family found itself and that of my family. Non-Jews had a choice; their Jewish fellow citizens did not. They were targeted by the Germans and were doomed from the start. My parents could easily have stayed out of the battle and could have avoided major confrontations with the German authorities; my parents-in-law did not have that option. Their range of choices was very narrow, even narrower than it seemed because of a bewildering array of decrees and exemptions with which the Germans were hiding their true intentions.

In retrospect, it is easy to criticize the decisions many Jews made. At the time, however, as news filtered through from the East, a great deal of confusion and disbelief prevented them from reacting adequately to the threats. Moreover, many Dutch Jews considered themselves to be Dutch rather than Jewish, and even refugees who had reached Holland felt loyal to their country of adoption. They may have hoped or expected protection from non-Jewish Dutch citizens. Even those who had an inkling of what awaited them had no idea how to react. Bruno Bettelheim's contention that Anne Frank's family should have resorted to armed resistance instead of passively going into hiding is absurd, and shows a total lack of understanding of the conditions that prevailed in the Netherlands under German rule. What objectively seemed the right reaction could turn fatal, while unwarranted risk-taking sometimes led to salvation. In the literature about the harrowing experiences of the victims of Germany's racial policies, survivors tell their stories, inevitably creating the impression that the will to survive was the key to success. Yet almost everybody wanted to survive, and many of those who died were as resourceful as the survivors.

Survival often depended on a willing helper at City Hall or on the discretion of a gathering where nobody asked further questions after a dangerous slip by one of those present. The fortuitous discovery of

Jews by a group of Dutch policemen searching for black-market meat could be fatal when the police lacked the courage to look the other way. Exceptionally, there were even Germans who, on an individual basis, softened the impact of the policies of their government. However, for the great majority of Dutch, German, and stateless Jews who lived in the Netherlands at the time of the German invasion, the "final solution" was indeed final.

Remembering Alex
1939-42

For a long time I believed that events indelibly imprinted on your mind became part of you. Among such events I considered those that took place during the short period of my great friendship with Alex, about forty-five years ago. However, recently, when after a particularly moving film that evoked many memories I could not sleep, and for the first time consciously thought of Alex again, I realized I was wrong: some images have remained clear, but far from forming a coherent whole, they seem to float in a vacuum, what comes before or after being blurred. I wondered if even the feelings of friendship, which I felt were unchanged throughout the years, were perhaps myth rather than reality. Did they still have a real content, or was an empty shell all that was left? In order not to lose what is still left and maybe even retrieve some of what seems to have disappeared, and above all, to protect, for myself, the authenticity of our friendship against unsettling doubt, I shall try to write down my classmate Alex's story.

Of the first year in high school (1939-40), when I turned thirteen, nothing has remained, except for the moment when Alex entered the classroom, on the day we were given our timetable. He was very obese, and he shuffled as if he was wearing slippers. His clothes looked faded and wintry, much too warm for early September. Strangest of all was his hair, which gave him the appearance of an old man, although he was only one year older than I was. It had probably been brown and curly, but now it was dull and very thin. The hair that was still left seemed on the verge of breaking off or falling out. When he said his name and gave his address, his voice was unexpectedly soft for somebody of his appearance. At home I told my family about the strange obese man whose name was something like Alexander Riem, and who lived in Zwanenburg, a village halfway between Amsterdam and Haarlem. I asked my father, who normally taught mathematics at an HBS, a high school without Greek and Latin, but who that year also gave a few lessons at the Barlaeus gymnasium, the high school I attended, if he could look up the exact name on the students' list. The name he found made my hypothesis of a farmer's son from the Haarlemmermeerpolder rather unlikely: Alexander Rimini evoked exotic places, not sugar beets and wheat fields.

In the course of the autumn I learned, although I never came into contact with him, that he lived at the Zwanenburgwal, in the very heart of the old Jewish quarter in the centre of Amsterdam. He was, therefore, likely to be poor and Jewish. I did not go beyond this observation, for I did not feel particularly attracted to him, although his deliberate and quiet way of expressing himself did impress me. He had one real friend, Kees Terpstra, a reserved boy of few words, and when the two were together, I thought them a dull pair

We did talk about the war once in a while in those days. I believed the Netherlands would stay out of it, yet I felt a vague uneasiness when the Germans invaded Denmark and Norway. The indeterminate anxiety about a possible catastrophe took a different form after the capitulation of our country to Germany, and I began to register in my mind who among our acquaintances and my classmates were Jewish. There were so many Jews in Amsterdam—some eighty thousand—that I believed the Germans were unlikely to do anything. The end of my first year in high school and the first summer of the war were relatively calm. It was possible to believe that the storm would blow over without serious damage, but in September the lull was over.

A ranting teacher of Greek represented the New Order. He introduced military discipline into his classes and extolled the virtues of the National Socialist way of life. We were taught German by a rancorous, colourless woman whom we considered suspect, not only because of the language she tried to teach us but because of the many comparisons she made between healthy, energetic workers and repulsive, loafing, silver-spooners. We nagged and teased her mercilessly, and after a few months she disappeared from the scene. We did not dare challenge the

Greek teacher. We whispered "jerk" and "bastard" so softly that he could not hear it, and that was all. Curiously, neither he nor the teacher of German ever showed any sign of anti-Semitism, and neither commented on the portentous developments of the fall of 1940. On the other hand, their restraint was not so curious, for those developments took place almost sneakingly—especially in the initial stage—because pretty well everybody involved felt too ashamed to talk about it.

I heard for the first time about the Aryan declaration[1] when my father discussed it with my mother. He foresaw the consequences of signing that declaration, and was of the opinion that everybody should refuse to provide any information at all. My mother agreed with him, but both were afraid that those who refused would be fired. That night I could not sleep and had confused visions of poverty and hunger. I finally decided that if everybody refused to sign, the Germans could not do anything, and then I tried to make myself believe that if everybody did sign, perhaps not very much would happen anyway. Everyone signed, and with a mixture of disappointment and great relief I understood that my father too had given in under the pressure.

Of the weeks that followed, little has stuck in my mind. I only remember the remark of a girl who was one year ahead of me. The year before, she and a couple of her friends had teased me because I was a teacher's son, but this time she was very kind and serious. "It must be strange for you," she said, "that your father is leaving our school, whereas you may stay." At first I did not understand her and said that my father would indeed be teaching full-time at the modern high school next year. She looked at me as if I were talking gibberish. "So he isn't leaving by the end of November?" she asked. Then it dawned on me what she meant. My father was very dark and not very Dutch in appearance, and I myself would not have been chosen for a photo-reportage in *Der Stürmer*, a German National Socialist weekly with vicious caricatures of Jews and pictures of healthy, strong, blond Aryan workers. "We aren't Jews," I said, almost apologetically, for she herself was Jewish. After a moment of awkward silence, she concluded: "Then you will both stay," and that was the end of our conversation.

1   A declaration that a person belonged—or did not belong—to the Aryan race, Aryan being used by the Germans as "Caucasian of non-Jewish descent."

At the end of November, both the vice-principal, Dr. de Vries, who taught Greek and Latin, and the biology teacher, Miss Biegel, a middle-aged woman with a great sense of humour, whom I liked very much, disappeared. In her place came a timid blond man with a soft, hesitant voice, upper-class pronunciation, and a classy name. Without any insight into human nature, we declared him a traitor and made life impossible for him. One day he tried to win us over by offering to read us a story from a book of what I would now call educational and authentic animal tales. The classroom for natural history was big and rectangular. At one side, on a platform in front of the class, was a demonstration counter, with the teacher behind it. We students were seated at long tables on trestles, placed parallel to the counter. "Read a story? Oh yes!" we exclaimed, pushing our tables a little closer to the platform. "Oh yes!" we exclaimed again and pressed onward towards the baffled teacher, who had risen from his seat. In the end, the front rows were almost crushed by the tables behind them. Only the very last table, which was fastened to the floor with bolts, had not been moved forward. Its students shouted for joy and waved to the pressing mass. Alex had tied his handkerchief to a ruler and used it as a flag. I had never seen him so exuberant. I had a warm feeling for him and thought he was perhaps not that dull after all. The principal, whose office was on the second floor just above the natural history classroom, came down and restored order. The teacher did not come back. Later we heard that he was "good," and about four months after he had left, a small group of us even went to his house to apologize. However, so many things had happened during those months that perhaps even in his view the story-reading incident was no longer very important.

So much has been written about the February strike that the myth created in the course of the years around it forms an obstacle to my own memories. It was the only mass demonstration of non-Jews to show their solidarity with the Jews; those were days when Amsterdam proved to be heroic, determined, and charitable. Today it is commemorated each year with a wreath-laying ceremony and speeches, but how much of it is still really remembered? As so often, the chronology of memories is lost. I recall isolated events—the death of a Dutch militia man, which triggered the first raids and deportations, and the closing off with barbed wire of the old Jewish quarter. The Weigh-house, one of the oldest buildings in Amsterdam where merchandise was weighed and measured in the olden days, was situated just inside the Jewish quarter, behind barbed wire barricades several metres high: did I see it myself, or is it an image I have appropriated, looking at picture books commemorating the war? I know for sure, though, that the first time I saw the barbed wire, whether it was near the Weigh-house or somewhere else, I panicked. What are they to do now? I whispered to myself. Was Alex—the only person in the Jewish quarter I knew—inside or outside the closed-off area? I do not remember. It would be easy to check in the archives of the municipality of Amsterdam, but what does it really matter? In any case, he lived very close to the centre of unrest in those February days.

Towards the end of the month, when the real strike erupted, the streetcars did not operate and the wildest of rumours were circulating; Alex's place in our classroom was empty. In the excitement over the strike, almost a flush of victory, his empty place reminded us that defenceless people were involved and that the battle took place in our immediate vicinity. The hated Greek teacher looked at the empty place and his enigmatic comment was: "That's what you get!" Nobody had the courage to ask him what he meant. He probably did not know himself, for that matter.

After two days, the streetcars were running again with armed Germans on the front platforms, and Alex appeared again in school. Amsterdam was punished with a huge fine, to be paid by the taxpayers in the highest tax bracket, but the barbed wire fence of what should have become the ghetto disappeared—either a small concession, or a clever move on the part of the enemy. I thought at the time this was a very important victory. I told Alex, with whom I had hardly had any contact before the February events, that I had thought of him a lot, which was true, and that I was glad to see him again at school. He was a little surprised, but pleasantly so, and said that all the drawbridges had been pulled up, and that everyone in the neighbourhood had stayed inside as much as possible.

This conversation could be considered the beginning of our friendship, yet it took six more months before we really became friends.

Towards the end of the second year of high school, rumours circulated that Jews would no longer be allowed to attend public schools, and that after the summer vacation special Jewish schools would accommodate them. Alex had not yet come to our house in those days, for it was in the last month before the vacation that my sister, who was sitting near the window, called to me: "Look, what a strange man over there, with a boy who's about your age!" When I looked, I saw Alex and his friend. For a moment I hoped they were coming to see me, but they continued on their way. "That's not a strange man, that's Alex," I said, and I realized I was so used to seeing him that the faded raincoat he wore, his obesity, and his baldness no longer struck me as odd. "He seems a nice guy," my sister said in a conciliatory tone, "but ordinary he isn't."

In all likelihood we would never really have become friends, in spite of my hesitant overtures, if his almost inseparable comrade had not moved to Utrecht in August of that year. Even then, our friendship almost didn't happen because of a difference of opinion about the conversion of our Greek teacher. With a select group of intellectual Dutch Nazis, he had gone to Berlin for a few weeks in the spring. As a substitute, we had had the principal's secretary, who had a degree in Latin and Greek, a fact that even at the time seemed unusual to me. We hated it when his return put an end to her friendly and relaxed lessons. But instead of the ranting and raving we expected would resume fortissimo, we heard thinly veiled apologies from him about mistakes that had been made, and promises that from now on things would be different. Later, we found out that instead of staying with the group all the time, he had gone exploring Berlin on his own. What he saw and heard on his expeditions in the city made him completely lose faith in the New Order. Part of our class was immediately willing to forgive the repentant sinner; others were more skeptical about the sudden change, and doubted whether it was sincere. Alex belonged to the second group, I to the first. For a while there was some friction, when the one group reacted too positively in the eyes of the other, or when the other group appeared too resentful. The controversy eventually solved itself: the pros lost some of their enthusiasm for a man who, although no longer a Nazi, had, like almost every teacher, unpleasant qualities; the antis were gradually won over, especially when it became clear that the man was not an anti-Semite.

After the solemn graduation ceremony with which the school year always ended, we went our separate ways. In spite of the situation, my parents had rented a cottage on the Veluwe again, a scarcely inhabited region with forest, sand dunes, and heath, about sixty kilometres east of Amsterdam, between Amersfoort and Apeldoorn. During the war Amersfoort gained notoriety because of the concentration camp the Germans built there. In Apeldoorn Queen Wilhelmina used to have her summer palace, Het Loo, with a vast area, the Royal or Crown Domains (that are part of the Veluwe), most of which was accessible to the public. There were occasional reminders even there of the war—German army units moving along the Amersfoortse weg, the highway from Apeldoorn to Amersfoort, and a gamekeeper who guarded the sections of the Royal Domains closed to the public, as if the Queen were still taking her private walks there, although now he was ensuring privacy to German hunting parties. Nevertheless, it was a wonderful vacation, even though we had more than our share of rain. Against my better judgment, I believed the rumours circulating before the vacation about a special Jewish school would probably prove to be false—the Germans would not take such a measure against children! Each time my parents, who were very pessimistic, discussed how worrisome the situation was, I had the feeling that Amsterdam was far away, and I was inclined to run away from them.

In September, Alex, Appie Davidson, Freddie Kijzer, and Robert Simons (his first name pronounced in the French way) did not return to school. Neither did Jan Dik Wiener, with whom I had been in the same class from the first grade of elementary school. On one of the first days of classes, I went to the new Jewish school to tell my former classmates that I would not abandon them. The new Jewish lyceum (a school with both a classical and a modern section) was housed in the building of an elementary school, opposite the orthodox Jewish modern high school, founded long before the war, and observant of Jewish holidays. It was in a back street and could be reached from the Amstel through a covered passage. I arrived precisely when school was over. An excited stream of students pressed their way outside. One could hear animated conversations and laughter. I was not the only one waiting for friends and former classmates, and there were many surprised and happy greetings.

In the crowd I discovered only Appie Davidson and Alex. Appie told me he did not have a Greek grammar, and I promised to ask the repentant Greek teacher if he could help. Appie indeed received that book, and that is all I did for him with all my good intentions, and yet it is more than I did for the other classmates, with the exception of Alex.

Not quite at ease, Alex and I walked alongside a canal. "How was it?" I asked. He laughed: "It's better than I thought, but it's a little bit much; only Jews, everybody talks and talks and talks. The caretaker is called Cohensius." "You gave him that nickname?" "No, it's his real name." At a given moment we stood still. "I must go home," I said. "Will you come with me, or would you rather come next time? Then you can tell your mother and stay for dinner." "That seems better to me...and you should also come to my house," he replied.

This was the beginning of what I remember as a very intensive relationship. Did we really go to each other's houses that often? Of Alex's first visit I have only kept the memory of the great, yet unobtrusive, kindness of my parents and of a certain relief on the part of Alex, who apparently had dreaded the encounter, although he had had my father as his math teacher and therefore knew him already. Maybe that was precisely the cause of his apprehension. I became acquainted with Alex's family shortly afterwards. I knew that his father had died and that his mother had remarried a widower with five children a few years later. All of them were what was called "slow learners," and Alex was clearly the odd man out. From what he said I understood that he got along with them fairly well and that they even looked up to him.

Did I go to meet Alex at his school or did we go from my house to his? What I remember clearly is how we climbed up some stairs together and entered a very dilapidated and messy maze of rooms and passages, full of ramshackle furniture and very dark. Everyone was curious to see Alex's new friend, especially the little ones, Sammetje and Fietje, who were both still in elementary school and looked at me as if I was some sort of wonder of the world. Herman, about the same age as Alex, was a slightly backward boy, whose speech was at the same time very fast, substandard and indistinct, so that I had trouble understanding him. He looked like his father, Sal Bromet, but the father spoke more clearly, although his voice was always hoarse. The oldest brother,

Harry, was much better looking, sturdy, with dark curly hair and regular features. He wore high rubber boots when he returned from work, and those boots also contributed to the general impression of strength. What work he and his father and Herman did was not quite clear to me. Lies, eighteen and a few years younger than Harry, but older than Alex and Herman, earned her own money, took good care of her appearance and was better dressed than the rest of the family. During this period they were more and more restricted in what they could do, yet after each new interdiction they managed with great ingenuity to think of something that could become a source of income. Sometimes they were busy in what could be called a home industry, as when the whole family cut out insoles and glued felt on them, to sell to a shoe manufacturer. Another time they painted and varnished hundreds of flowerpots. They gave me one for my mother. It had running green, brown and yellow paint, a real eyesore that we kept for years without using it, but lost when my mother moved after my father's death.

Except for Alex, they all had the Amsterdam accent, Alex's mother less so than the rest of the family. Almost immediately after our first greetings she asked me whether my parents had no objections to my visiting them, and she was visibly moved when I said that this went without saying. I did not like her reaction, yet I felt flattered and had a sensation that must have been well-known to ministers' wives delivering soup to the poor. I do not think I realized at that moment how desperate and abandoned by everybody they felt. The resourcefulness with which they absorbed each new blow, and the energy they directed to the solution of even minor inconveniences during the first months that I visited Alex's house, presented the illusion of an indestructible will to live.

In that respect, too, Alex was out of tune. In the course of time he had bought a collection of history books from second-hand dealers at the Waterlooplein market around the corner from his home. From reading them he had come to believe that in the global course of events the individual does not count, and that what is usually called a positive outcome always comes too late for a great number of people. Proudly he showed me a row of books on a shelf behind a curtain, but in spite of his assurances that I could always borrow them, I never did. Once or twice I quickly leafed through the works. Most dated from the nineteenth century; the print was often small, and the language—mostly Dutch, but also German and English—solemn. His plans to become a strategist, something he spoke about on our walks through the city, did not appeal to me either. A strategist had to deal with armies and war, and I did not understand exactly what Alex wanted to do in such a vague, but definitely military, profession. In retrospect I wonder whether I really knew him.

The friendship with Alex remained completely separated from my normal school existence, although we sometimes discussed homework and recent school events. I do not believe that Alex ever joined us on a class outing or was even invited for a class get-together at somebody's house. It was as if we felt that our world and his no longer fitted together. Besides, combining those worlds was growing more and more difficult, because much of what we did was forbidden to Jews. Once during the winter of 1941-42, I went skating with a large group of classmates on a flooded sports track, the Sintelbaan, at the Olympiaplein. The day was bitterly cold and the window of the ticket booth was completely frosted over. Because children younger than ten were allowed in for ten cents instead of the quarter everybody else had to pay, we bent our knees when buying our tickets and cheated the Sintelbaan out of fifteen cents. This was very easy, for the lady in the booth could not see us. When we went to the skating rink, however, I was tapped on the shoulder by two policemen who were posted near the entrance. They wanted to see my identity card. I was fourteen, one year under the age set for having a compulsory identity card ready to be shown at any moment. "I don't have one," I said, truthfully. "How old are you?" one of them asked in a stern voice. Completely panicking because I thought they had noticed the cheating, I answered: "Fourteen." "That's a lie," he said, "You're a Jew, and you're not allowed to be here." My classmates, amazed, had followed the exchange from a distance, without understanding what was the matter. "No," I said, "I'm here with my classmates from the Barlaeus Gymnasium. You can ask them." They now came closer and also stated that I was not a Jew. The policemen shrugged their shoulders and, only half convinced, let me go. "Hi, Moshe!" my friends called, "Come, hurry up!" Strangely enough, the incident took on the quality of a heroic act, and I felt that my solidarity with Alex was stronger than ever. He too liked the story very much, and if he felt that instead of bringing us together, what had happened highlighted the enormous distance separating us, he certainly did not say anything in that vein.

In the spring, Alex talked more and more often about a possible separation. As an unemployed Jewish worker, his brother Harry had been sent to Geesbrug, a work camp in Drenthe, in the northeast of the country. I wrote him a letter without knowing what to write, and when he replied that he was doing fairly well, but that hunger was a big problem, my mother sent him a parcel with rye bread and liverwurst. Whether it ever reached its destination and whether Harry was still there I do not know, but chances are that he received it. Alex was convinced that his turn would come too, and my counter-arguments that the war would long be over before it came to that had a more and more hollow sound.

One day he confessed to me that he had not felt at home during our second year at the gymnasium, and had avoided the superficial classmates who were interested only in school parties. He added: "I thought you were one of them too, but there I was terribly wrong." For me this confession was wonderful, and I felt very close to Alex, and yet I could not keep up with him as he rapidly matured. While he was trying to prepare himself mentally for a journey to the menacing unknown, I went on my bicycle to the island of Texel, the most southern of the Frisian isles, where we had spent many summer vacations, but which had been declared a military zone. Only those under fifteen could go there without a special permit. It was during the Easter vacation and I would turn fifteen in May. Alex had had his sixteenth birthday in March and said he could not have joined me even if he had not been a Jew. I sent him and his family a letter and went to see them soon after returning to Amsterdam, full of enthusiastic stories which I now think would have been better kept to myself.

Shortly afterwards, the order came that all Jews must wear a yellow Star of David, and I stopped talking about Texel to Alex. Many rumours circulated about non-Jews who, out of solidarity, wore the yellow star, but there was nothing like a mass demonstration that might have cancelled the effect of the German measure. What was intended was achieved: the Jews were even more isolated and vulnerable than before. Some people even let their Jewish friends and acquaintances know—sometimes delicately, mostly not—that they were, of course, always welcome, but it would be best not to wear the star, and certainly not in broad daylight. My parents were very indignant about that kind of attitude, and our friends continued to come as usual, although "as usual" is not the right expression.

Alex too kept coming regularly, and we continued to walk through the city after school at least once a week, but usually more often. We talked about tests and translations, compared marks and the amount of homework each of us had, but it was a facade behind which we were hiding our fears. By the end of June the facade collapsed and we had to face reality. The Germans had started to call up Jews aged between sixteen and thirty-two for work in Germany. I remember very clearly how, on a summery evening, Alex and I crossed the bridge of the Staalstraat and turned into the Zwanenburgwal to his house. All of a sudden, resonating over the water of the canal, we heard a prolonged scream, swelling in waves, a cry of distress or of lamentation. With a bang, the open window from which the scream had come was closed. Startled, I stopped and looked, asking Alex: "What is this?" He pulled me quickly with him and said in a nervous, almost grumpy tone: "Oh, I'm sure they must have received a summons there. One hears this kind of scream often in the neighbourhood." We now walked in silence to Alex's home, which was close by. With a sigh of relief we saw that Sammetje and Fietje were tidying up the room, while Alex's mother was in the kitchen warming up something. Everything was normal, precisely as it always was. Three days later Herman, Lies, and Alex were called up for work in Germany.

A very busy and confusing period began. Continual efforts were made to find a hiding place for Alex and the two others, while at the same time the preparation for their departure took its inexorable course. Alex and I were almost inseparable; I accompanied him every day on his expeditions, after which I often went home with him. There were all sorts of things that had to be done before leaving. Later the Germans operated much more quickly and the administrative part of the process was no longer intended to give the impression that those who were taken away to work in the East would be able to keep in touch with those staying behind. For the first transports, the Jewish Council not only made lists available of what could be taken but also provided much of what figured on the lists. The fact that letter paper and writing tools were mentioned induced people to speculate that things "over there" might not be that bad after all. The decree that everyone must have his picture taken was strange; we did not understand the real purpose of those photos, which was to make the deportation look like an official emigration. Herman and Alex went to a Jewish photographer in the Kalverstraat who gave them a couple of extra prints for free. Both gave me one of them. On the back of Alex's photo was written: *Quis separabit*. I did not understand the meaning precisely, but did not dare ask. Did he want to say that nobody could separate us, or did he wonder who would depart? Herman had written on his picture, "Thou friend Herman." "Thou" had a solemn ring for him, and it moved me then as it still does now. Lies had gone to a different photographer, and for the occasion she had donned a black party dress of shiny material she had just bought, with a wide skirt and puffed-up sleeves. Her photographer had not given her extra prints; to remember her, Lies gave me a small, earlier snapshot in which I could not recognize her very well.

Apart from the obligatory pictures, my friends were required to go to some administrative authority to sign declarations renouncing their Dutch citizenship. Beforehand, Alex and I had discussed at length whether it was possible to refuse, because without the protection of Dutch citizenship, one was much more vulnerable. When the document was put before them to be signed, there was no way out and they had to obey the order. Alex told me that he had written *v.c.* under his signature—*vi coactus*, compelled by force—and that nobody had noticed, but that in this way his signature had become invalid. For a moment we were delighted; he had outwitted the Germans. Soon, however, fear for the future dominated again.

People did not yet talk openly about going into hiding; it seemed a taboo that could be broken only with great caution. From only half-formulated reactions of my parents and from Alex, I had the impression that they were ready to give him shelter, but shrank from taking three

Jews into their house, of whom two, Lies and Herman, were total strangers. Alex had a strong sense of solidarity, however, and I doubted if, when his stepbrother and sister were sent away, he would be willing to stay in Holland. My sister and I especially tried, sometimes in consultation with our parents, to think of addresses where Lies and Herman could hide. Together or separately we rode on our bicycles through Amsterdam to various reliable friends and acquaintances, but only a former cleaning lady with a sweet wrinkly face, who originally came from the countryside, was willing to let them sleep for a few nights in her two-room apartment in the Jan Pieter Heyestraat, if they had nowhere else to go. All the others had, in their own eyes, very well-founded reasons not to give hospitality: neighbours who could not be trusted, their own poor health or that of a member of the family, too little space. After four days we gave up: people were afraid to take Jews into their homes because they were threatened with extremely harsh punishment if they did so. A further complication was that the Germans had warned those who were to be sent off that, if they did not show up at the given time at the indicated place of assembly, their families would be held responsible. If the missing Jews were discovered, they would be sent to a concentration camp. Going into hiding thus was not only a practical problem but also a moral dilemma.

The Tuesday morning of Alex's last week we were sitting with my sister in the only light corner of our dark and gloomy living room. For the umpteenth time we were talking about the risks involved in not showing up. "And yet," my sister suddenly said, "you must not go. Over there, in Germany, they'll kill you all." "Yes, I know that," Alex said quickly, as if he had not wanted to hear it. His voice had sounded irritated, and I was angry with my sister for having expressed her opinion in such a brutal way. Moreover, I thought, things would definitely be less awful than she presented them. I do not remember how the conversation evolved, but that evening I cried bitterly. My father stroked my head with his hand, but he did not say a word.

The next day and evening I must have done something, although I do not know what. School was over, but the official graduation was still going to take place. That Wednesday Alex and I did not see each other. The next morning I heard that my mother, having discussed the matter with my father, had gone to the Zwanenburgwal in the evening to offer Alex shelter. Alex had been very grateful, but he did not want to abandon Lies and Herman. Moreover, he was afraid to put Sammetje, Fietje, and his parents at risk. The uncertainty was over, and there were only two days left before the departure of the transport.

In Alex's house there was a strange, feverish mood. Clothes were washed and mended, piles of underwear were lying around, eating utensils were sorted out, provisions for the trip were prepared. Alex had put aside, for me to take home, a few books he particularly liked, some silver guilders and two-and-a-half guilder pieces in a small box. I put everything in an old canvas bag, in which I had brought homemade bread for those who were leaving. With the promise to return the next day I said goodbye, not knowing what more I could do or say to help. When I was passing over the bridge of the Kloveniersburgwal, I saw a *Grüne* (German military policeman in a green uniform) standing on the bridge. I felt a mixture of hatred and fear, but I was also for a moment, for a very short moment, attracted to him, wanting to explain to him that Alex should stay in Amsterdam, and that he should protect him and Lies and Herman. He signalled to me to come closer and, pointing at the canvas bag, he asked: *Judengüter?* (Jews' goods?) I whispered, *Ich verstehe Sie nicht* (I do not understand you), whereupon he remarked that I had said that in German all the same. My voice was even softer still when I said: *Das habe ich in die Schule gelernt* (I learned that in school). He looked bored and made a gesture that I could go. At home I told about the incident as if it was a heroic feat, but I said nothing about the flash of foolish hope. My parents were happy that things had ended without harm. They said I should have said *in der Schule*, but that it did not matter.

The last evening, like all partings, was not easy. Alex's mother cried silently and said she wanted to put an end to her life. His father caressed her hand and whispered, "Liene, Liene." His voice was even huskier than usual. Lies said to me in a low voice: "She won't do it, I'm sure. She's too much of a coward." This remark, which no one else heard, was the only discord I perceived, but the tension was almost unbearable that evening. Herman responded to the tension by playing the clown. At a given moment he buckled on his backpack, put on a cap, and marched through the room shouting: "The Jews are going to conquer Poland!" Everybody laughed. Sammetje and Fietje looked at him, full of admiration, and his mother smiled through her tears: "What a boy!" With the solemn promise to write each other as often as possible and with a big hug, we took leave of each other. Alex gave me a big envelope with a letter he had already written in September, and which I promised, after reading it, to give to his friend who had moved to Utrecht. The entire family waved goodbye to me when I crossed the bridge of the Staalstraat. That same night Alex, Herman, and Lies departed. The next day I went to a summer camp of the Netherlandic Youth League for the Study of Nature one day later than the other participants. A friend from a higher year, who had also stayed in Amsterdam out of solidarity with me, accompanied me to the camp.

When I returned to Amsterdam, a message from Alex had just arrived from Westerbork. He described how they had left the train in Hooghalen early in the morning and had gone on foot to Westerbork, their baggage being transported by trucks. The camp was terribly crowded and everybody had to help. "I must now do kitchen duty," ended the postcard written in pencil. I found it difficult to write something in return, yet I did, although we doubted Alex was still in Westerbork. I went to see his parents, and when I was on vacation that summer I wrote them letters that I signed, "Your almost son." There was no news from Germany or Poland. Although the call had been for work in Germany, people spoke only of Poland, just as Herman had that last evening.

In the early fall, during one of my visits to the Zwanenburgwal, I heard that Alex's father had to go on a small boat every day to the other side of the harbour to work. He was tired and more restless than ever. The deportations and street raids were turning the family's life into a hellish nightmare. In October, Alex's mother told me she had been rounded up with Fietje during a street raid and taken to the Hollandse Schouwburg. There Fietje had started to cry uncontrollably and an older German felt pity for them and took them out to the street via a back door. Fietje and Sammetje, one on each side leaning against their mother, were listening with wide-open eyes to a story they must have heard many times already. Father Bromet was not back yet from the other side of the harbour. When I came again in November the house was empty. Slowly I walked home, and from then on I avoided the Zwanenburgwal.

When, shortly after the liberation, I happened to be in the neighbourhood, I took my courage in both hands and went to look. For a moment I had a shock of joy; on Alex's floor the lights were on. However, when I came closer I saw that it was the house next to his, and that his house had disappeared. During the famine winter of 1944-45, people looking for firewood had demolished it.

The Fortune Teller
1936-43

It is more than thirty years ago since Corrie and I left Amsterdam with our two young children; our third child was born in Princeton. At first we planned to stay away from Holland for one year, then a few years, but in the end we realized that we had become immigrants in Canada, the country to which we moved after two years in the United States. Our ties with our country of origin have remained solid, yet we do not completely belong there any more. We have adopted all kinds of customs and social conventions of Canada—we have lived in Toronto for more than twenty-eight years now. Canadian holidays too, at first without meaning—Thanksgiving, for example—have become a real tradition, while Ascension and Whitsun, Dutch holidays, have completely disappeared. Birthdays are no longer what they used to be in the Netherlands, where one must remember the birthdays of relatives and friends, visit them with a present, or at least give a phone call. All important birthdays are marked on a birthday calendar, hung in the bathroom so the risk of forgetting is minimal. After we moved to North America, we noticed that the birthday person feels slightly let down on the great day, but in general it is a relief no longer to live under the constant pressure of the birthday calendar. Only Saint Nicholas Eve we still really miss. Presents were on the whole much smaller than the Christmas gifts in North America, but more personal. They were accompanied by a poem written by Saint Nicholas or his helper Black Peter, in which the recipient was either mildly teased, or praised and thanked for something he or she had done for the givers whose identity must be guessed. Although we try to keep up the tradition with surprise packages and poems, chocolate initials and marzipan piglets, we never completely succeed. This is partly because a few weeks later Christmas must be celebrated. When all of North America is unwrapping presents, one should not make the mistake we made the first year of taking a brisk walk with the children to enjoy the outdoors instead of exchanging Christmas gifts like everyone else. Thus we remain ambivalent: to be Dutch and faithful to old traditions, or to become Canadian, making new customs a habit? We muddle on and remember, full of nostalgia, the real Saint Nicholas celebration of olden times, which becomes more beautiful as the years go by.

And yet next to this idealized image, there is for me the painful reality of a Saint Nicholas Eve, more than half a century ago, vividly remembered in spite of the time that heals all wounds. The episode of the miniature Gouda cheese also comes to the surface, equally embarrassing, although at the time it happened it seemed insignificant. Both the Saint Nicholas memories and the Gouda cheese are closely connected with my eldest brother Kees's best friend.

Kees was a peculiar boy who kept to himself, what psychiatrists would call a borderline case. As a child he had strange fantasies that he wrote down in small exercise books, in the form of stories. He stopped writing when he was in high school, yet at that time, too, he must have lived half in a world outside reality. Seven years older than I, he was already in high school when I started elementary school. Apart from physical education, he had almost all top marks, and when encouraged by my parents, he talked with them about his schoolwork. He had only two friends. One friendship went back to elementary school, and in high school he again made friends with only one boy. Because his first friend had gone to a different school and contact with him was less frequent, the new friend soon became the more important one. I do not remember very much about the first years when Johan Jacobs came to our house. From pictures I can reconstruct that he already wore glasses with thick lenses because he was nearsighted, and his shorts almost completely covered his knees, which in those days indicated that the wearer was an overprotected mother's boy. The first friend, Wim, wore the same kind of shorts and also had glasses, though less strong. Both were pampered only children with few friends, a detail that struck me much later.

It did not take long for my parents to like Johan. I think anybody who became friends with Kees was automatically in their good books. On his side, Johan extended his friendship with Kees to include all of us, my two sisters, my brother Jan and me, and my parents. He lived in a stately house near the Concertgebouw. I was inside his house only once, and felt very intimidated. I do not believe I saw his father on that occasion; perhaps he was already ill. I remember that his mother, a rather heavy woman, had a sad face, with the corners of her mouth pulled down. It is possible that our first encounter fixed this image in my mind, but later encounters would have had the same result. Anyway, I never saw her cheerful. Before Johan had finished school, his father died. I do not know whether Johan had already left the modern high school by then and enrolled in the commerce school, but the change of school did not have any impact on his friendship with Kees and after his father's death he came to our house even more often than before. His mother and he had moved to a small third-floor apartment, too small for the large pieces of furniture from their previous house. I thought it must be terrible to lose your father, and I tried to be extra nice to Johan.

The next few years are almost without memories of Johan. Too many things were happening in my own family. First, in 1936, my brother Kees had to be admitted to a psychiatric institution because he could no longer distinguish between terrifying hallucinations and reality. After a few months, when he came home again, my eldest sister, Ynske, a year and half younger than Kees, fell ill. Ynske had always been very sweet, and spoiled my second sister and me, buying us chocolate bars and candies and letting us taste the excellent results of her culinary art. But then she refused to eat and grew terribly thin. My parents tried everything, and even took her and Kees on a cruise to Norway, promising us other three children our turn would come. A few weeks after the voyage, at their wits' end, they went with her to a psychiatrist on the day before school started again. On the first day of school, when students were given their timetables, she suddenly became very ill. She was rushed to a hospital, where she died after five days. I was ten years old and did not understand how all this had happened. I had the feeling that something in my life had been irreparably destroyed.

Whether Johan knew all the facts I will never know, but I do remember that in those years, when dark sorrow and self-reproach made our house unattractive, he was one of our most faithful visitors. He helped my—now only—sister Elisabeth with her homework. At a school dance, I was told, the other pairs left the dance floor in order to give Johan, who was an enthusiastic dancer, and my sister free room for the intricate dance patterns he executed with great skill. People had called, "Keep going!" and when the dance was over everybody applauded. My sister, who was about fourteen at the time, said that she had not liked the applause, but for Johan it had been a triumph. He loved modern dances and everything modern. He often used fashionable slang, a habit that must have irritated my parents who were very language-sensitive. I remember a formula my mother used more than once, with respect to Johan: "Oh, Johan, he has brought no evil into this world." It was, I think, a sort of conjuration to suppress the irritation he provoked. At the time I did not understand this, but I did wonder whether it was nice—or rather not—to say about somebody that he had not brought evil into this world.

After the war broke out, and especially after the Germans invaded our country, it seemed as if my parents were waking up from years of introverted mourning and were beginning to pay attention again to the outside world. They were among the few people who, even in the beginning, were pessimistic, although in the summer of 1940 everything looked fairly harmless, except for the destruction caused by the five-day war in May. My parents did not want to go on vacation, but "the children," that is to say my two brothers, my sister, and I, together with Johan and one of my sister's friends, Trees Duijts, who was a few years older than Elisabeth and already working in an office, were going to make a bike tour. The six of us formed a very unusual group of cyclists. None of us had ever gone on a bike tour before, we had never stayed at youth hostels, we did not have small flags attached to our bicycles, and nobody had a guitar or a recorder to play near a campfire. Although our mother had purchased chequered wool shirts for her three boys, we did not completely fit in. By far the most bizarre was Johan, who wore

The parents Schogt with their children from left to right: Ynske, Henry, Kees, Elisabeth, Jan. Amsterdam, 1928

a navy three-piece suit. It was a good opportunity to wear the suit, he claimed, and as an extra advantage he could put our Youth Hostel membership cards and our money in its inner pockets. Of course, he sometimes wore other clothes, but the navy suit made him into a curiosity. Soon, a few days into our trip, some to whom he had explained the advantages of his curious outfit, nicknamed him "the secretary," and during the rest of our trip we were often saluted by fellow hikers with the exclamation: "Hurrah! the secretary with his suite!" At first I felt a little ashamed, but later I found it rather amusing.

It was a wonderful excursion, particularly interesting because of what we saw in the region of the Dutch Water defence line, which had turned out to be completely useless in the five-day war against the Germans, and exciting because of rumours about a youth hostel father (manager) who was said to belong to the Dutch Nazi party. In the new circumstances created by the Occupation, I was aware that both Trees and Johan were Jewish, a fact to which I had not paid attention before. For me, those were secondary matters and, as a typical thirteen-year-old boy, I was happiest about the fact that we came through provinces where I had never been before. What was new too, for me, were the half-hidden tensions that arose because Trees had designs on Johan, who in turn was courting my sister without much success. Making smart-alecky, precocious remarks, I showed I had noticed, and because people laughed I repeated myself once too often, until I was told I had made my point and should stop. I can still feel the shame and humiliation of being put in my place: accepting criticism has never been my forte.

Two other events on that trip, in which Johan played a major role, have also made an indelible impression on me. The first took place when we were swimming in a brook near the Yssel River. It must have been in the second week of our tour, for Trees, who had only a one-week vacation, had already returned to Amsterdam. We had discovered a deep water hole where we could not touch the bottom. Johan, who could not swim very well, tried a few strokes. He was sniffing and snorting and his head was sagging, half under water. "Just like a sinking frigate," Elisabeth remarked, and Jan quickly took his camera to keep this image for posterity. But suddenly my sister exclaimed, "He's drowning!" and jumped into the water and pulled him ashore. Johan sat shivering in the sun, and nobody laughed any more.

If there had sprung up a feeling of protective solidarity with Johan near the brook, that feeling was totally nullified by what happened near the village of Oldebroek, a few days later. It was a muggy, hot day. The last stretch before our return to Amsterdam was fortunately short, from Epe to Oldebroek. However, we had to bike up a hill, the Woldberg, which was quite a climb for bicycles without gears. An ice-cream vendor had strategically chosen a position near the top of the hill at the side of the road. When asked which flavours he had, he answered: "Vanilla and Summer Delight." We wanted to know what Summer Delight tasted like, because it was a flavour unknown to us. The man gave us a scrutinizing look and stated hesitantly: "You don't belong to the enbas." Only Kees knew that NBAS was an acronym for *Nederlandse Bond van Abstinent Studerenden* (Netherlandic League of Abstinent Students), and so he could say to the vendor that he had guessed right. Then came the laconic explanation: "Rum, but they're not allowed to have any, so I call it Summer Delight." We laughed about it, and the ice cream was delicious, but the youth hostel was fully occupied, all places being taken by the abstinent students. Back to Epe, where we could not stay either. It was late in the afternoon, and tired irritation was now mixed with fear: where could we go to sleep? Agitated, Johan said he perhaps knew a place, and he disappeared to make a phone call. A moment later he was back: "The Elekinds in Nunspeet can put me up, but Georgina is at home and it would be too much if all of us came. Two is possible, so Kees, do you want to come with me?" Kees preferred to stay with us and Johan left with a "See you tomorrow in Amsterdam," heading for Nunspeet. Georgina was a girl of about sixteen who had Down syndrome. I had met her once or twice during a previous vacation on the Veluwe. I wondered whether Johan had really asked for shelter for all of us, or whether he had made up the Georgina excuse afterwards. We were very angry, even Kees, and with a feeling of great solidarity we rode through the Royal Domains to a family we had known as neighbours the summer before, when my parents had rented a cottage in Hoog-Soeren, not far from Apeldoorn. They took us in with great kindness; that night there was a fierce thunderstorm, and the next day in cool, sunny weather we cycled back to Amsterdam. I was furious with Johan, who had abandoned us.

My parents' only comment on Johan's behaviour was that in difficult circumstances not everybody can be a hero. However, I kept a grudge and openly began to react to everything that bothered me about Johan: his sea lion-like laugh, his habit of stating the obvious, and his tendency for repetition to avoid silences. It is highly likely that I had caught some suppressed negative reactions of other members of the family and subconsciously counted on their approval. With my first remarks in the vein of: "Did I hear that already before?" or "When is feeding time for the sea lions?" I earned a few half-hearted smiles, but soon this was finished, and what I myself thought to be smart and witty, everybody else found annoying.

Most of the time Johan himself acted as if he had not heard anything and ignored my spiteful taunts. On rare occasions my parents intervened: once when coming home from school I commented on Johan's presence in our house; my father asked me to stop it, saying that Johan would always be welcome in his house, regardless of what might happen. I understood that he not only put me in my place, but also made a statement against the Germans, and I did not like to be thought of in the same league as the Germans. This happened in the spring of 1941, after the February strike, when Amsterdam stood up for the Jews. It had not stopped the Germans, however, and the measures against the Jews were no longer at the stage of secretive preparations. I really wanted to start with a clean slate and succeeded more or less when Johan came to stay with us for a week in the country, on the Veluwe in a house across from the Echo pit, five kilometres west of Apeldoorn. The fact that we were more outdoors than indoors in spite of endless rain, and also the fact that Elisabeth, who had found a real boyfriend shortly before the vacation, was no longer followed by Johan everywhere, had considerably eased the usual tensions. After a week, Johan returned to Amsterdam on his bicycle. In the letter in which he reported his safe return home, he wrote that he had become so wet in the pouring rain near Baarn that the sign "Restricted Freedom of Movement for Jews" had seemed superfluous to him: his clothes were stiff and glued to his body. In spite of the humour, the letter called forth an oppressing picture of a dripping-wet, rain-soaked Johan, alone in a hostile environment. Being sharp and mean to such a person was reprehensible and despicable.

    Back in Amsterdam, even with all my good intentions, I relapsed into the old patterns. I was really happy when an occasion for reconciliation seemed to present itself around the eve of Saint Nicholas. Elisabeth and Jan told me in secret that Johan, who was going to celebrate the evening at our house, had no less than three packages for me. It would be nice if I also gave three presents to Johan. I had already bought him a piece of inferior marzipan fashioned to look like a chunk of bacon, and after the conversation with my sister and brother, I bought Johan a pocket diary for 1942, and two deep-fried croquettes, also of marzipan, but this time of excellent quality, from a pastry shop. Things had almost gone wrong with the croquettes, but that was not Johan's fault. When it was finally my turn in the crowded pastry shop to say what I wanted, I was asked to my surprise to wait a moment. Finally, I received two hot, round meat croquettes in a paper bag. In the shop I did not have the courage to protest, and I did not want to take them home either, for fear of being ridiculed. The only solution was to eat them, hidden in a doorway. It was a big sin, for in those days I was a vegetarian, the only one in our family. The next day I went again to the pastry shop and was more successful. So much trouble would certainly be rewarded, I thought. But things worked out quite differently.

As always, the poems formed the most important part of the Saint Nicholas celebration; as always the poet himself was listening most intensely when his poem was being read, ready to intervene when the wrong rhythm or clumsy deciphering of an almost illegible passage threatened to spoil a well-chosen pun. Sometimes a surprise present made up for the lack of poetic inspiration, while the present itself clearly had to show the good intentions of the giver.

> Johan, croquettes are good for you
> I don't give one, I give you two.

and

> Saint Nicholas found in his yard
> For Johan this chunk of bacon lard.

were not great poetic art. I really did not know how to deal with Johan. As for Johan's presents to me, their message was clear enough. The first package was enormous, it contained a smaller one that contained an even smaller one and so on until all that was left was a tiny box that was empty: "Your well-deserved award." Halfway through the evening, as a variation on this theme, I was given the traditional birch broom for naughty children:

> In Saint Nick's books you get the lowest ranking
> And for your behaviour a good spanking.

Everybody liked the joke and laughed. It was not easy to be a good sport, yet I succeeded in joining in the laughter, albeit out of the wrong side of my mouth. The third package, in which contrary to all reason I hoped to find a real present, was the last straw:

> You are not funny but a bore
> Who gets half a cent and nothing more.

I was very angry with my brother and sister who must have known Johan's intentions, when they urged me to do something special for him, and fuming against Johan who had made such a fool of me. I opted out and no longer took part in the fun. The next afternoon there was a small paper bag for me on which was written: "Careful, breakable!" It contained two eggs. The previous night Saint Nicholas had forgotten to give them to his young vegetarian friend whom he really did like. "How nice of Johan, his rations for two weeks! Now you see that he means well, after all." Thanking and accepting thanks was not easy, but after these formalities the air cleared somewhat. The clashes—always provoked by me—did not occur any more. In the first months after the ill-fated Saint Nicholas Eve, I avoided Johan as much as possible.

In the course of 1942 it became clear that "Restricted Freedom of Movement for Jews" had only been the beginning and that far more was at stake. After the introduction of the yellow star and the first transports via Westerbork to the East, the street raids started and the nightly removal of Jews from their homes began. There was no room any longer for negative personal feelings: help had to be given as much as possible. In retrospect, one could divide the reactions of the victims under threat into three categories. Many people, especially in the first months of the *Auswanderung* (emigration), complied with the order to show up for deportation to a labour camp, some hoping to be strong enough, others without illusions. Other people went into hiding, sometimes because one of the family had been ordered to report for "resettlement," often without having received an order. Finally, a large group tried to get a postponement or an exemption by legal means.

Trees Duijts belonged to the first category. On a sunny day in September, she came to say goodbye. She was not strong: a minor heart condition and poor blood circulation made her chances of surviving forced labour very slim. She knew this very well, yet she reported. She did not want to endanger the lives of her mother and one of her two brothers, whose first child had just been born. I had never before given her a kiss, but that day I kissed her. I see her trembling chin and her face, tensed into wrinkles, before me even now. The happy bicycle trip of two years earlier seemed to belong to another era, to another world.

Johan fell into the category of those who would try anything in order to be allowed officially to stay in Amsterdam. First he believed that a doctor's declaration, stating that he was flat-footed and extremely nearsighted, would provide sufficient protection. When it appeared that such documents were worthless, he tried to obtain a so-called Calmeyer exemption. Proof had to be provided that two grandparents were non-Jewish. Johan based his hope on two small oil paintings of his grandmothers, both wearing Frisian headgear, as he never got tired repeating. Delicately, my parents tried to make him realize that rural costumes did not prove anything, but for a long time he clung to this new straw. He even consulted a lawyer who, according to my sister, kept him on a string and, as was to be expected, did not get anywhere. It may have been the influence of his girlfriend, but slowly he became more and more inclined to go into hiding. His relationship with Betty probably started in the early months of 1943. Betty was from an upper-class Jewish family with a long Portuguese name, and she was very nice. She did not visit our house often, not wanting to create unnecessary risks for my parents, although they completely disregarded the interdiction against receiving Jews—an act considered hostile to the occupying forces. Because the Portuguese Jews were temporarily exempted from deportation, she was not in immediate danger, and she therefore worried even more about Johan.

With a poorly faked identity card in the name of a certain Aloysius—or maybe Jacobus—Wanrooy, Johan came to live with us in August. He hoped to get a better identity card from the acquaintance who had provided the Wanrooy one, but when Ton van Leen finally came, she brought Johan only a miniature Gouda cheese that still had to mature and a few cans of condensed milk. She was a heavy-set woman, with short blond hair and a flat, pale face, a sort of unbaked pancake. When she talked with my mother about the situation, I noticed that she did not finish her sentences, but let her voice die away with a drawn out: "It is aaawwwful," or "One cannot imaaagine," while raising her eyes to heaven. I thought she was theatrical and exaggerated, but now, half a century later, and more aware of what was going on, I do not think she was. She left, promising to return as soon as she had a better identity card for Johan. This promise she kept, unfortunately.

Whether Mr. Brouwer—"just call me Brouwer" (a privilege I found difficult to use)—was a contact man for Johan, or visited us for some other reason, I am not able to verify, searching the depth of my blurred and incomplete memories. He visited our house a few times, during and after Johan's stay. Mr. Brouwer was a cheerful man of around thirty, with a crewcut. He did the "heavy work," transporting people who had died in hiding in a small boat to a remote spot on one of the lakes near Amsterdam, where he committed his load, made heavier with stones, to the waters. He was firmly convinced that the Germans would lose the war, and after one of Mr. Brouwer's visits, everyone took heart again.

Johan, however, soon lost courage and often he sat with his head in his hands, sighing softly, "Oh, my God! Oh my God!" I felt really sorry for him, yet his complaining irritated me, since he was well-off compared to those who had been deported. It did not dawn upon me that "relatively good" could still mean "very bad": Johan suffered from being locked up, from constant fear, and from being totally dependent. My parents and my sister did their best not to give him that feeling, my father called himself the *postillon d'amour* when he took a letter from Johan to Betty and vice versa, and my sister maintained contact with Johan's mother, who, resigned, awaited her fate, and could not be persuaded to go into hiding.

This situation, in my recollection, lasted much longer than, objectively, could have been the case, but it ended abruptly when Ton van Leen brought a new identity card. Immediately Johan wanted to go outside again. My parents believed this was far too dangerous, especially because he had walked in the neighbourhood fairly recently, wearing the yellow star. When Johan stated that he preferred to rent a room in another part of the city rather than be cooped up, they tried to make him realize that this too was very risky. After a few days they gave up, and Johan left. I was relieved that the tension was over. In the afternoon—Johan had gone in the morning—my sister and I happened to be in the cellar. "Look," I said, "all Johan's cans are gone, but he didn't take the cheese." "It's mouldy," she noticed, "maybe it's spoiled." "Let's scrape off the mould," I suggested, and went to the kitchen to fetch a sharp knife. We scraped, and some real cheese showed under the mould. We tasted it; the cheese was excellent. The cut cheese looked very strange, though, and we did not know how to get it back into shape. So we went on carving and eating until nothing was left. We probably ate more than a month's ration. We threw the mouldy crusts into a public garbage bin down the street. That evening we said that we had thrown the cheese out because it smelled awful and was spoiled. For a moment my mother, who had a worried and preoccupied expression, looked up: "What a pity; you didn't know, of course, that under the outer layer it wasn't bad at all." There was no further discussion.

Johan found a room in the western part of the city. Three days later Elisabeth met somebody who asked her if she was still in touch with Johan Jacobs. He was almost certain he had seen Johan at the station in Bussum, running to catch a train that was already moving. On a visit to Johan in his new room, Kees learned that Johan had indeed gone to Bussum to ask the director of the small accounting firm where he had once worked whether he could come back. "We must sternly urge him to be more cautious," my mother sighed, "Running after a train, drawing everybody's attention, what was he thinking!"

A few days later Johan came to see us, in spite of my parents' request that, for his own safety, he not visit us. He was a nervous wreck. Betty's father had heard that his *Sperre* as a Portuguese Jew had been declared void, but that he would be put on another list which, like the previous one, provided temporary protection. In extreme anxiety he had gone to the German headquarters for Jewish resettlement to find out if that was true. He was informed that the first list had indeed become void, but that his name had not yet been added to a new list. He was not on any list, they concluded, so they detained him. Betty and her mother had also been taken from their home. Johan had consulted a clairvoyant, or fortune teller, who had assured him that he would see his girlfriend again within two weeks. This reassurance had given Johan some hope that Betty's father would manage to persuade the Germans to let him go. There was little uplifting that one could say, and nobody had much confidence in the fortune teller. My father accompanied Johan part of the way to his room. He had declined the offer to stay overnight with us.

The attempt to obtain the release of Betty and her parents failed.

They disappeared to Westerbork via the Hollandse Schouwburg, from where the Amsterdam Jews were taken to the Central Station by streetcar. Shortly afterwards, Johan was arrested. Mr. Brouwer, whom he had been able to contact, and who himself had access to one of the Germans who guarded the Schouwburg, told us that Johan had gone to the fortune teller again. He had apparently assured him that he really would see Betty again shortly. After the consultation, when he left the fortune-teller's house, German policemen were waiting for him. "But he had such a good identity card," I said interrupting Mr. Brouwer's account. "That was not much help when they opened his fly," Brouwer said. I felt foolish; it was the first time that I had heard about this method of detection. Brouwer's contact man was going to be on duty again in two days. Soldiers had to be bribed; the contact man would try to smuggle Johan out of the Schouwburg and hand him over to Brouwer. An amount of eight hundred to a thousand guilders was needed, and evidently success was not guaranteed. For my parents it was a large amount of money and they did not know what to do, mainly because it would be difficult to find a permanent way to help Johan once he was free again. What they would have ended up deciding is an open question, and afterwards the dilemma was never even mentioned; Johan, in the category singled out for special punishment, had been sent almost immediately to Westerbork before Brouwer's contact man was on duty again. In Westerbork, Johan and Betty saw each other, indeed. The fortune teller had made sure his predictions would come true.

Johan's mother, one of the last Jews who had not gone into hiding, was taken from her home. A neighbour who wanted the apartment for some friends had drawn the attention of the authorities to the fact that Amsterdam was not yet completely *Judenrein* (free of Jews). Betty came back from Auschwitz in 1945, the only survivor in her family. After the war, the fortune teller was sentenced to a few years in jail. A mitigating factor was that he had denounced only a few Jews, and had done so to avoid having to work in Germany.

Mr. Rozenberg's Cigars
1932-45

Sometimes, due to unusual circumstances, people who do not belong to the circle of close friends have a greater impact on the course of our lives than their relative position warrants. My parents did not have many intimate friends with whom to share their deepest thoughts. The Rozenberg family did not qualify for this small inner circle, but they were what one calls good acquaintances, whose presence at birthday gatherings was taken for granted. They had lost an infant son. Later a second son was born, whom they called Freddie. During the war the contact between the two families intensified with far-reaching consequences.

My earliest memory of Freddie Rozenberg concerns an incident that took place on my birthday, my fourth or maybe my fifth; in any case, I was not going to school yet and even Freddie and my cousin Lida, who were both one year older than I, were not yet in first grade. A small table and three little chairs had been set for us and we were sitting there, each with a pastry in front of us. My cousin and I kept a watchful eye on each other and each other's pastry, afraid of finishing before the other, who would then still have a piece left.

Freddie, who had wolfed his down, fidgeted restlessly on his little chair. When Lida, who had won the competition in self-control with flying colours, pensively moved her pastry around on her plate in order to enjoy her triumph as long as possible, Freddie suddenly grabbed the pastry, pushed it with force into her face, and shouted: "Child must eat pastry!" Lida burst out crying, the mothers intervened, saying soothingly that Freddie had only wanted to help—which I doubted even at the time—and the children's party was hastily ended.

Freddie was a bit taller than I and had dark curly hair and a friendly face. Only his eyes were never at rest; he fell over his words and sometimes he burst out laughing without any visible cause. When I went to his house and played with him, something his mother very much encouraged, we would race through the apartment or I would build a tower with his blocks. He would watch me for a short while, but soon lose all interest. The cookies, chocolates, and fruit drinks tasted much better than at home, and I liked Freddie, although I found him very strange. But I often felt bored because nothing really happened, and so, when we were older, I stopped playing with Freddie and he no longer came along with his parents when they visited us on birthdays. He was enrolled at that time in a small class for mentally disturbed children. There, with endless patience, they taught him how to read a little bit. Arithmetic was apparently less difficult for him.

Freddie's father was, like mine, a teacher of mathematics at the Fourth Modern High School. Mr. Rozenberg, small and pudgy with a pinkish face, wore three-piece suits. His hair curled a little if it was not too short, and through the years more and more of his scalp became visible. His most striking feature, however, was his left eye, which looked off in a completely different direction from that of his right eye with which he looked at the class. His students said it was difficult to use cribs in his class, because they never knew if they were in his field of vision. He was strict as a teacher and more than once he asked my brothers and my sister, who went to his school, who was the second-most feared teacher there. He was visibly pleased when he was named. The most feared teacher was Mr. de Boone, a man with a personality disorder who maintained a reign of terror in his Dutch and history classes and who turned out to be a member of the Dutch National Socialist League during the war. Unlike Mr. de Boone, Mr. Rozenberg was an excellent teacher, totally committed to the work he believed to be very important. My father often seemed lost in daydreams and did not adapt his abstract way of thinking to the level of his students; much of what happened in his classes he did not notice. Yet, in spite of their different styles of teaching, Rozenberg and he—they called each other by their last names—liked and respected each other.

My mother thought Mr. Rozenberg rather a bore, but she had a soft spot for his wife, who was very fat and talked so fast that she almost stumbled over her own words. She had a sweet face, usually with a worried expression, no doubt because of Freddie's condition. Her name was Vrouwtje (Little Woman)—or at least that is what it sounded like to me—and I thought it was rather peculiar that such an enormous woman was called Vrouwtje. I called her so, too, and she thought this was cute. When one day my mother reminded me to say, "Mrs. Rozenberg," Vrouwtje smiled and said, "Let him," and thus it always remained "Mr. and Vrouwtje Rozenberg."

They were faithful birthday guests. I still see them sitting with the other grownups around the table in our living room, with tea and cookies or coffee with cake. I would listen to the stream of words coming from Vrouwtje, whose Groningen accent sounded funny, without hearing what she said, and watch the enormous cigar Mr. Rozenberg always smoked. My father had no respiratory problems, but he thoroughly disliked what he called the stench of cigars and cigarettes, and consequently we were not allowed to smoke in the house, nor were our friends, who were asked, rain or shine, to go to the garden to smoke. When I had reached the age when a casually blown cloud of smoke indicated that you were part of modern life, I found that restriction annoying and embarrassing. However, there were always exceptions, and Mr. Rozenberg, who seemed almost addicted to his Havana cigars, was one. Shrouded in a cloud through which one could see his pink, walleyed face, he fascinated me long before I myself became of smoking age.

This somewhat smug contentedness did not last very long after the Germans had invaded our country. The Rozenbergs were afraid and bewildered, and came for advice to my parents, who were as powerless as they but less directly threatened. I suppose the Rozenbergs took all sorts of financial measures in time, for during the entire war my father looked after their interests and made payments when necessary. There was nothing secretive about it, although my parents did not say very much; there were more important and more difficult problems. When his father was no longer allowed to teach at the Fourth Modern High

School, Freddie hardly noticed the change, although he must have felt some of the worries and fears of his parents. Unfortunately, it did not take long before Freddie was directly affected by the German decrees preventing Jewish students from being in the same schools as non-Jews. His teacher tried to obtain an exemption for him, and she kept him for a few weeks in her class in spite of the negative answer she received. Eventually his teacher and parents became too afraid, and Freddie stopped going to school. From then on the Rozenbergs were, in effect, prisoners in their third-floor apartment at the end of the Johannes Verhulststraat, with fewer and fewer possibilities to break the tedium of forced idleness. Once in a while Freddie escaped onto the street and wandered aimlessly around the neighbourhood.

One afternoon, returning from school, I found Vrouwtje Rozenberg in the living room. She was visibly upset, talking even faster than usual. My mother, who sometimes listened only with half an ear and once, during an endless phone call, had even held the receiver at a distance, at intervals saying "yes, yes," to show that she was following the conversation, was very attentive this time. Freddie, who did not understand why he could no longer go for a walk in the Vondelpark, and angry because their telephone had been cut off, had accosted a German soldier and reproachfully told him that he wanted to go to the park and that their telephone should be connected again. The soldier, not understanding very much, had given Freddie a friendly pat on his shoulder and continued on his way. Of course, one could not count on such a favourable outcome a second time. Although he was already fifteen years old and not small for his age, his mother tried to create the impression that he was still a child by giving him shorts and childish clothes to wear. But officially he had to carry his identity card with the ill-fated J at all times, "and we can't keep him inside all the time either," Vrouwtje said. My mother sympathetically accompanied her part of the way home, but she did not know how Freddie could be protected either.

Both my parents helped as much as they could. My mother bought vegetables and fruit when greengrocers became out of bounds for the Rozenbergs, and each time my father visited the Johannes Verhulststraat, he took valuables home to store them until better days would come, or to give to the Rozenbergs in an emergency. Much of what he brought home was non-perishable foodstuffs, neatly stacked on a separate shelf in our cellar. To which category the Havana cigars belonged was not entirely clear. The supply seemed almost inexhaustible, and next to the big bookcase with sliding glass doors in my father's study, a part of the wall disappeared behind boxes of them. I had the impression that they became a source of mild irritation. First, a shawl was put over the boxes by way of camouflage; later, everything was hidden behind a Persian rug that also came from the Rozenbergs.

To my shame, I must confess that I did not follow very attentively what happened to Freddie: my schoolwork and my friendship with Alex, who had been forced to enroll in the Jewish high school in September 1941, almost entirely monopolized my attention. Freddie was not completely out of my thoughts, though, and in the days after the yellow star became compulsory, I asked my father what Freddie's reaction had been. He said that Freddie did not want to wear the star, and yet it was impossible to keep him inside, as Vrouwtje had explained earlier. Fortunately, they had managed, with great difficulty, to get Freddie accepted in the Apeldoornse Bos, a Jewish institution for the mentally ill, where he would be safe. I felt relieved, but was very sorry for Freddie, who had to live in an institution far from his parents. "Does he have to wear a star over there?" I asked, just to say something. My father said he did not know, but presumed the star was compulsory there, too.

According to the first news from Apeldoorn, Freddie was very restless, often asking when he would be allowed to go home again. But when the first transports went east via Westerbork, everybody was grateful that he had not stayed with his parents. Each time new measures were introduced, we thought the nadir had been reached, and each time it turned out that things could get worse still. When the Germans started to block off entire streets and drag the Jews from their homes, mostly at night but sometimes in broad daylight, my father could not take it any longer. One afternoon when we were all at home, he asked us to come to the front room for a moment.

Originally this room had been my grandmother's drawing-room. She was a stately woman from the east of the country who had invested her money in Russian railroads and lost it. Even before I was born, she was living with us. Over the years our whole family preferred her drawing-room to our living room, which was very dark even in the middle of the day. In 1942, she was in a very advanced stage of senility, always sitting in her grandmother's chair and continually packing and unpacking the contents of a little basket: old keys and all sorts of odds and ends. She had become very kind-hearted, and accepted whatever happened to her. Strangely enough, I do not remember whether she was present at the gathering my father had called; she had almost become part of the entourage, so that one did not notice her any more.

As always, my father spoke slowly and with caution, formulating his sentences carefully and without superfluous words. The Jews' lives were in danger; he did not trust the labour camps in Poland; the Germans were capable of anything. "Mother and I would like to open our house if we are called upon," he stated, finishing his brief exposition, "but as there is serious danger involved, for you, too, we cannot do this without your consent." Without hesitating we gave our consent and I had the feeling of having been present at a solemn event.

Not much happened in the first weeks after the family council, until one day my father arrived, walking hurriedly through the Obrechtstraat, together with the Rozenbergs. Street raids were going on in the neighbourhood and there were rumours, as people said in those days, that it was the "turn" of the Johannes Verhulststraat. This meant that all the houses where Jews lived would be systematically searched. Still wearing his coat with the yellow star sewn on it, Mr. Rozenberg stood in front of the window, looking out into the street to see if there was any trouble. Gently, my mother pulled him back, saying that it was not advisable to show himself so openly with a star. That night they stayed with us, together with Johan Jacobs, a friend of Kees's who lived in the Cornelis Krusemanstraat. Johan's mother had preferred, as he put it, to stay at home. An exercise was held in which the three fugitives had to lower themselves through a trapdoor in the floor of a walk-in closet in the living room, where the china for festive occasions was stored. A few cushions and blankets had been put in the narrow space under the floor. It was quite a production that took a considerable amount of time, and speed would be crucial if the hiding place were needed. Fortunately, the rest of the day and the night went by without any need to use the emergency refuge. After my father had made sure the coast was clear—he had taken his bike to go to both the Johannes Verhulststraat and the Cornelis Krusemanstraat—the guests left again for their homes, for they had not yet thought of going into permanent hiding. Mr. Rozenberg had only one kidney and thought that invalids would be exempted from forced labour, once they had received a *Sperre* from the Germans, which gave them protection from what the Germans called resettlement. It was at this time that Johan Jacobs developed his fantastic plan to prove that both his grandmothers had been Aryans.

I was proud of my parents without realizing what the tensions had been like for them. Of the fall of 1942 I do not remember much, except the feeling that what happened around me could not be true. In a few months, more than half our Jewish acquaintances and friends disappeared, but I did not let it sink in and dreamt that my former classmate Alex, who had been taken away in one of the first big transports, was coming back again. In January, however, the last illusions that things in Poland were perhaps not all that bad were shattered. Confused stories came from the hospital in Apeldoorn, according to which the Germans had decided to clear out the whole institution, but the administrators had flung open the doors before their arrival. Some patients had left the buildings, but had returned towards dinnertime and fallen into the trap; others were still wandering through the woods, if they had not been sheltered by charitable neighbours. Without waiting for further news, my father immediately left for Apeldoorn with a glimmer of hope that he would find Freddie. After a day of searching, during which he heard gruesome details of the German operation, he returned home empty-handed, cold, and dispirited. He looked precisely as he had on that day a long, long time ago, when he returned from the beach on the island of Texel, after a storm, with a few shreds of the tent in which we used to change. That had not been a catastrophe, and my mother had said we could easily rent one of the wooden cabins. This time she started to cry softly, saying she hoped Freddie had been killed immediately after crossing the border, instead of being killed in Poland after a long train ride, locked up in a cattle car.

Those first days I could not think of anything but Freddie and the fate that had befallen him, but soon our family became preoccupied with new problems. The Germans demanded that university students sign a declaration of loyalty; otherwise they would be refused access to classes. My brothers needed no time to arrive at a decision: signing was out of the question. This meant that my brothers had to go into hiding, which would not be easy for Kees, the eldest, because of his vulnerable unworldliness, but he too left for an unknown destination, just before two police officers in civilian clothes came to take him and my brother Jan at half past seven in the morning. They ordered my father, who was shaving, to dress quickly, and took him to the police station. Against all expectations, he was released that same morning after he had truthfully declared that he did not know where his sons were. In the afternoon, he went to school to teach.

After a couple of weeks, Kees came home again. The East Groningen minister who was in charge of a network of hiding places had given up after several farmers who had sheltered Kees had asked the minister to come and take him elsewhere. The distance between the farmers, who were not used to city dwellers, and Kees had been too great. Kees did not ask them to call him by his first name; when asked whether he would like to eat in his room or with the family in the kitchen, he chose to eat alone. In his mind, he was given the choice, and he did not realize that he should have eaten with his hosts. One family after another found it too awkward and difficult to have such a strange and uncooperative guest. After this failed attempt to go into hiding, Kees did not want to look any further for a hideout, and, when he received an official summons to present himself for work in Germany, he left for Ommen, not far from the German border, with a group of students, among them my sister Elisabeth's boyfriend. They were to stay there for some time and would then be sent to various destinations in Germany. Thanks to the intervention of a psychiatrist who had treated him when he was in his fourth year of high school, and had sent him to a psychiatric hospital for several months, Kees received an exemption at the very last moment and was allowed to return to Amsterdam. He had to sign something suspiciously similar to the declaration of loyalty, but nobody ever mentioned this. Elisabeth, who was deeply disappointed that her boyfriend had gone to Germany and was working in a factory and thus helping the Germans in spite of her pleas not to respond to the summons, became even more involved than before in illegal activities, an important part of which was to find shelter for Jews.

One day, she asked if she could bring a year-old baby into our house. The child was in hiding with her mother somewhere in the centre of the city, near the Haarlemmerdijk. The mother was foolishly careless and the contact persons had judged it safer to take the child away from her. "What a harsh measure," my mother said. "Is it really necessary?" My sister told her that in spite of repeated warnings, the mother had again been spotted in a café. Changing her tone of voice she added: "It goes without saying that I shall look after the child." Although my mother understood that an important part of the care would come to rest on her shoulders, she immediately consented. And so, in early June 1943, shortly after her first birthday, Marja came to our house.

She was a very beautiful baby, with dark curly hair and big brown eyes. She was extremely pale and lay motionless in her pram. Her father had been caught in a street raid and sent to the East when she was two months old. Soon after, her mother had gone into hiding. Since then, Marja had not been outdoors. Although our garden got little sun, squeezed between houses that were four stories high, she was often outside in that month of June. She had not been with us for even two weeks when a monster raid was organized and the Germans searched for Jews without skipping a house. My aunt, Lida's mother, phoned at half past five in the morning to say that she had had "visitors" and thought they would probably "visit" us too. At her house everything had gone well, and she hoped the same would be true for us. The Germans had started their raids near the stadium in the extreme southwest of the city, and were moving from west to east, systematically combing one neighbourhood after the other. It was a nice, summery Sunday, but there was hardly a living soul in the street. We sat in the garden with Marja in her pram. I was amazed by the calm of my parents, bordering on fatalism, and tried to imagine what would happen if the Germans came and wanted to take away the little baby. I could not picture it, though, not even as more news reached us about the thoroughness and the brutality of the raiders who, if a door was not opened quickly enough, bashed it in and, once inside, searched and upset everything.

When the raids had moved to the east end of the city and evening had fallen, it became clear that our section of the city, near the Concertgebouw, had been skipped for some reason. The Rozenbergs, too, had for the umpteenth time narrowly escaped, but the agonies they had gone through tipped the balance, and shortly afterwards, provided with false but very good identity cards, they moved to a pension in the Anna Vondelstraat. How good those identity cards were became clear when, accompanied by my father, they had been to see a doctor on the Willemsparkweg. On their way back through the Vondelpark, they were stopped and asked to show their identity cards. Fortunately, it was very dark that evening, and according to my father, the Rozenbergs had kept their calm very well. We saw even less of them now that they were in hiding. Once in a while my father took cigars to them—I do not know whether they were used as barter or smoked by Mr. Rozenberg. The question was too unimportant to dwell on. Other events completely took up our attention.

These events followed each other in rapid succession, even though it seemed that time progressed exceedingly slowly while we were waiting to be liberated. In Russia, the Germans were defeated at Stalingrad, but in occupied Holland they continued their reign of terror in the summer of 1943, as if nothing had changed. In July, we heard that my brother Jan had been caught during a raid in the house of his host, who was heavily involved in underground work. Jan was being held in the Scholtenshuis, a notorious police post in Groningen, where my parents would be allowed to visit him before he was sent to the transit camp in Amersfoort. They dashed off and, because my sister who, after the university was closed had taken a job as assistant pharmacist, worked the night shift, I stayed alone with my senile grandmother, Kees, who was not much help, and the little baby. On top of it all, our cleaning lady, who had worked for us for ten years, had announced a few months before that she could not come any more. Her husband, an unemployed steelworker with communist sympathies, had died in 1942, and it had become too burdensome for her to come to us every week from the other side of the harbour. Mrs. Bloem had three children, a son of my age, a daughter who was one year younger, and an "afterthought" about eight years old whom she had brought along when he was an infant. When she gave him her breast, I always watched full of interest, and she had never sent me away. After Mr. Bloem's death, the daughter had taken a job in a pub, and the household chores rested entirely on Mrs. Bloem's shoulders.

My parents' absence gave me a crash course in baby care. I actually liked looking after Marja, who had become much livelier. I was scared, though, that she would become ill after I had given her a bottle of milk that had turned sour—there was no other available at that moment—without daring to ask anybody if doing so was dangerous. By the second day, I was coping much better, but when my grandmother had a light stroke, I was at my wits' end. Fortunately, my cousin Lida's mother came to check if everything was all right, and my parents, whom she alerted, came home a day earlier than planned. Life took its normal course again although, after her stroke, my grandmother was even more infirm and completely incontinent.

In late July, Kees's friend Johan Jacobs came into hiding in our house, making my parents' heavy burdens still heavier. Johan left again, against their wishes, towards the end of September. In December, Mr. and Mrs. Jacobs (no relation to Johan) took his place. Initially, they were to stay only for a week until they could return to the address where they had stayed, which had been declared temporarily unsafe because somebody who knew about it had been arrested by the Germans. The Jacobses were very kind people, and after two weeks, when there was still no message indicating that everything was safe again, their departure was no longer discussed and they continued to stay with us. It was the first time that I came to know Orthodox Jews. Mr. Jacobs was a contemporary of my parents, about fifty years old, and she was nineteen years younger. They had a small son, even younger than our Marja, for whom shelter had been found in Rotterdam, a month after his circumcision. They had simply gone into the street, when the major raids that had passed over our neighbourhood had reached the area of the Oosterpark, where they lived. It had happened in the evening and, leaving behind almost everything, they had fled to acquaintances. After a whole day of roundups and house searches, even the Germans were no longer thorough, and they did not discover the Jacobses.

The identity cards they had later been given in the names of Franciscus Wiggerman and Sebilla Nipius came from the south of the country and looked slightly messy. In the spring of 1944, Karel, their contact person, came with safer, authentic-looking papers with the same surnames and they were "rejoined in matrimony," at which occasion we had a festive meal. My mother tried to respect the Orthodox kitchen as much as possible, but, of course, we did not have separate sets of china for milk and meat, with an extra-special set for Passover. I was then in my fifth year at the Barlaeus Gymnasium, and at an age when I tried to criticize other people's opinions, especially those of adults, proud to be such a smart debater, not realizing how inconsiderate I was. Once I asked Mr. Jacobs, whom we called Uncle Wiggerman, or simply Uncle—his wife was not Aunt Sebilla, but Aunt Bertha, her real name—what Jews did north of the polar circle when the sun set on a Friday and remained below the horizon for several months. It was the only time he became impatient and angry, saying that it was a silly question. I did not agree with him at all and wanted to pursue the matter, but my parents put a halt to the discussion, stating that there were more important problems than Sabbath at the North Pole.

In general, the rapport with the Jacobses was excellent and their presence gave meaning to our existence, as tangible proof that resistance against the persecution of the Jews was possible. Little Marja, who began to talk and walk quite early, was a source of joy and provided welcome distraction, for Uncle and Aunt Bertha as well, who terribly missed their own son. They never complained about it. Uncle, who spoke with an Old Testamental lilt, was the epitome of modesty and equanimity. That equanimity was badly needed, for all the time new complications arose, threatening to have far-reaching consequences.

In early February 1944, my grandmother died. The last weeks before her death had been particularly trying for my mother, with the continuous changing of bed linen and the washing of soiled sheets by hand in the bathtub. She remained patient and gentle, and her mother-in-law appreciated this so much that one day she asked my father, "Who is that very nice woman, Joop? Don't you think we should give her something?" The evening before she died she was so well that she came downstairs for dinner. After a solid meal of kale and mashed potatoes, she declared: "I really enjoyed the kale," and collapsed, her mouth distorted. Those were her last words; she never regained consciousness. In March, a grey-looking man in a raincoat rang the doorbell and said that he came from the housing bureau. Because one of the inhabitants of the house had died, a room had become available, and we would have to billet a municipal worker; he would like to have a look at the room himself. An old friend from the island of Texel happened to be staying with us at the time, and he was taking a nap in my grandmother's room. My parents persuaded the man from the housing bureau to come back later and to give them three weeks' respite. A member of the resistance who had a job at the municipal registry was alerted, and the storm blew over; evidently he deleted our house from the list of addresses where rooms were available.

It was in the same period that my brother Jan suddenly appeared, emaciated and with his head shaven, after taking a horse-drawn cab home from the Central Station. After having suffered in the Amersfoort camp from scarlet fever, dysentery, and diphtheria, he had been declared *arbeitsunfähig* (unfit for work) and sent home. Among other things he brought home a package of butter my parents had managed to give him in Groningen; it had been confiscated upon his arrival in the camp and had had more than seven months to turn rancid. Of course, many people brought other things for him to eat, and my cousin Lida and her girlfriends worshipped him as a hero. I was, admittedly, slightly jealous, but nevertheless very happy he was back. Everybody was home again. We even had a hiding place for our refugees made by a carpenter and a mason, themselves in hiding, who accepted work only in bona fide houses. The mother of Rob van Schaik, who had become one of my best friends, and in whose house they had built a wonderful secret closet, had recommended us. This gave us a feeling of being safe. Perhaps we would make it till the end of the war.

That summer, Aunt Bertha seemed to grow heavier all the time. I was undoubtedly the last to draw the right conclusion. My parents must have known even before the Normandy invasion. Although they foresaw complications, for them it went without saying that the Jacobses would stay and must be helped as much as possible. My mother thoroughly disliked contraceptives, while my father was very tolerant in this matter and of the opinion that everybody was free to do what he or she wanted. Their everyday behaviour did not change, nor did Uncle's. Only Aunt Bertha, originally from Germany, who had always tried to be optimistic, now definitely forced herself so that her slight German accent became more noticeable. As the chances for liberation became more real, her voice became more normal again and it sounded completely natural when, around Mad Tuesday, 5 September 1944, she said with tears in her eyes, "Our child will be born in a free Holland," and kissed my mother.

After the false hopes of Mad Tuesday, the battle of Arnhem took place and the allied advance was stalled. Suddenly, we were sucked into the dark hole of a winter without warmth and almost without light. Already in September the Germans raided a high school and took away the boys of the highest grade for the *Arbeitseinsatz* (work program). After that, we, the grade six boys of the Barlaeus Gymnasium, eighteen years old, and in our last year of school, decided no longer to attend classes. In the beginning the girls took work home from school to give to the boys, but this did not continue, homework not being a priority in those days.

When gas and electricity were cut off and there was hardly any coal left in the shack in the garden, running the household became so difficult that everyone became involved. The daily effort to keep things more or less going must have been exhausting for my parents, but they did not show it and tried to keep heart. During the first months of that winter of 1945, when we were without a radio, the feeling of being powerless was somewhat lightened by clandestine news bulletins. My sister Elisabeth had already taken an active part in drafting texts for and distributing the *Vrije Katheder* (Free Pulpit, a left-wing publication with communist leanings), but now my brothers and I became involved too. Even Kees one day declared he wanted to deliver a bulletin to his friend who lived nearby in the Gerard Terborgstraat. "Oh, could you then put one in the Elderings' mailbox as well?" he was asked. The Elderings were our upstairs neighbours; their front door was in between our front door and the gate in the brick wall that opened onto our garden from the street. While everyone had his or her own fixed route for delivering bulletins, the neighbours were not on anybody's paper route, and often they received their bulletin a day late because none of us had thought of them.

Precisely on the day when Kees had overcome his fears and wanted to do his share, the Nazi brother of the Elderings' domestic help had prepared a trap. There was a skirmish, and they took Kees away in an armoured car that had been waiting farther down the street. The next day my parents were notified that he was being held in the Euterpestraat at the headquarters of the SD, the *Sicherheitsdienst* (security police). Erna Kropveld, a friend of my sister, said that she would ask the mistress of Aus der Fünten, one of the highest-ranking officers of the *Sicherheitsdienst*, for help. Once in a while she could ask him a favour, and she had contacts with the Resistance movement. This seemed a wild story to my parents, and although they trusted Erna completely, their expectations were minimal. When, two days later, an important SD man was shot, the Germans by way of reprisal burnt down two villas on the Apollolaan and executed twenty-nine prisoners. At first it did not dawn on me that Kees could be among them. An only partially overheard conversation about whether they had taken the victims from the Weteringschans prison or from the Euterpestraat, and where precisely Kees might have been at that time, was an eye-opener. In the following days my parents waited for the news of his execution. One afternoon I found my mother sitting alone in the front room—something that rarely happened—deep in thought. "Mother, are you thinking of Kees? Was he in the Apollolaan…or are they sending him to a concentration camp?" I blurted out my anxieties before her. "I don't know," she said very softly, "if they have shot him, then…." She did not finish her sentence, but said after a moment of silence: "Poor Kees, he would have had such a difficult life, and now he won't." Was this her way of preparing herself for the worst, or was she convinced that Kees was not alive? I cannot answer this question even fifty years later.

After ten days Kees was home again. One of the legs of his trousers was in tatters, bitten to shreds by two dogs they had let loose on him the first day. He had been interrogated several times, but they had not beaten him. He told us they had asked him if he knew his mother's friend thanks to whose intercession they were letting him go. To answer yes had seemed wisest to him. My mother made a round loaf of rye bread and steamed it in an empty rusk tin; Erna was to give it to Aus der Fünten's mistress on behalf of my parents and Kees. I had the reassuring feeling that the Resistance movement was watching over us, and I believe the miraculous end of Kees's adventure gave everybody renewed courage. He gave ten guilders to the *Vrije Katheder* the day after his return, but did not venture outside as a "paperboy" any more. The fact that brother Jan's relationship with one of Lida's classmates "had not remained without consequences" hardly affected the general mood. And so we continued, mostly absorbed by material worries and by the chores of every day, until Saint Nicholas Eve.

All of us were in the dining room, which was small, damp, cold, and dark. It had a cupboard and a walk-in closet, and two French doors opening onto a space that used to be a veranda but had been closed off by a brick wall with windows, and given the grandiloquent name of conservatory, although it was not a healthy place for plants. The usual presents and poems of Saint Nicholas Eve were absent, but my mother had made an effort to put a proper meal on the table so that everyone was in a festive mood, even though we were sitting half in the dark, the only light coming from a tiny wick floating in a layer of oil on top of water in a jar. When there was a loud knock on the door, for a moment it seemed as if it was going to be a real Saint Nicholas Eve, somebody leaving a present on the doorstep. But the knocking continued and became menacing. When my father opened the front door, two armed German soldiers forced their way into the house with a man in civilian clothes who also spoke German.

One of the soldiers posted himself at the entrance to the dining room, but paid so little attention that Uncle was able to escape into the garden by way of the conservatory. He was a real closet-scholar, yet he climbed over the fence and hid behind shrubs in the neighbours' garden. Aunt Bertha stayed in the conservatory, hoping, if need be, to reach the living room and the closet with the open trap door. In the meantime, my father was ordered to show the intruders where his study was. By way of explanation they added: *Die Zigarren von hinter dem persischen Teppich, schnell, sonst nehmen wir das jüdische Kind mit* (The cigars from behind the Persian rug, hurry up, or else we'll take the Jewish child). The Persian rug was no longer in the study, and the cigars had been put somewhere else, but they did not seem to notice, and with their loot, consisting of a few boxes of cigars given them by my father, they left as quickly as they had come.

There was no time to recover from the shock. Clearly, somebody must have denounced us and our house was no longer safe for our friends. It was past seven, and after eight nobody was allowed outside. I do not remember how Uncle got to his contact address, but I know that my sister took Marja, the only one the Germans had mentioned, to a friend she knew from the Resistance. Aunt Bertha, who was almost due—the baby had already "dropped" (an expression I found mighty interesting at the time)—went with my father to a clinic in the vicinity of the Vondelpark. The next day, on 6 December, Dorus Wiggerman, who should really have been named Isidoor Jacobs, was born.

The house was eerily quiet without the people in hiding. For the first few days, we peeked outside furtively as if the raiders might come back at any moment, and we spoke almost in whispers. My parents thought, however, that the raid had not been ordered by the authorities, but was a private initiative. They suspected that Mrs. Bloem, the cleaning lady, had betrayed us, or had at least given us away inadvertently. The fact that the Germans knew where the cigars had been hidden in 1943 and had no knowledge of the presence of the Jacobs family pointed in this direction. "Perhaps they will come back for more," my parents worried. They did not come back, and after a week, fears had returned to pre-raid levels, kept in check and in the background, but there was a constant feeling that something terrible might yet happen. The homecoming of Aunt Bertha with baby Dorus—the somewhat feeble attempts to find a safer place for them had come to naught—was an almost festive reunion. The day before, Uncle Wiggerman and Marja had returned, and it looked as if nothing had happened.

For a while, the preparations for brother Jan's wedding with our cousin Lida's classmate, Fransje Kettner, occupied almost all our attention. In early January, wearing tails and a top hat that was too big, he went on foot to the City Hall with his bride, who wore a short white fur jacket. They were followed by a tired, shuffling procession of relatives, for it was cold and it took almost an hour to reach the Oudezijdsvoorburgwal. On the first of January, however, the impending marriage had been temporarily pushed to the background by what we thought was an emergency. My father had gone to the Rozenbergs with his best wishes for the New Year, and to see if there was anything they needed. He had found them in a state of utter agitation. About a week earlier a new butler had made his appearance in the pension. That morning, when bringing them their breakfast, he wished them the Hebrew *Mazel* and *brocha*. They pretended not to hear, but now wanted to leave the pension as soon as possible. My father promised to come back that same day, although he could not think of a quick solution. The Rozenbergs knew about Marja, but had not been told that the Jacobs family lived in our house. Perhaps they counted on being offered shelter there by my parents.

After a brief consultation it was decided to advise them to stay quietly where they were. If the butler really wanted to denounce them, he would not have warned his victims with a New Year's wish. He had probably wanted to show them that he was not fooled. Many people were like that, not realizing what it meant for those concerned about being discovered. Likewise, the head of the maternity clinic had asked Aunt Bertha the day she went home whether she was perhaps an "Israelite." By the choice of the expression she probably wanted to indicate that she was not anti-Semitic and Aunt Bertha had, uneasily, answered in the affirmative. "The man may also want to blackmail them," my sister suggested. "If he starts along that line, they must leave immediately." That afternoon I accompanied my father. If there was some trouble I could turn back. What my father and I agreed upon exactly I do not remember, but I believe I went together with him into the Rozenbergs' room. They were sitting huddled together at a large window covered with a sheer curtain. Dusk had set in already, but I could still see enough to get an impression of the heavy, solid furniture. They looked so lost and sad that I barely had the courage to say Happy New Year. After the conversation, held in a whisper, about the possible implications of *Mazel* and *brocha*, they seemed somewhat cheered up. They could come and stay with us—how, I wondered—should the butler ask for money. Should this happen, they would give it to him and then leave the pension without taking clothing or anything else with them.

What everyone hoped would happen did happen, that is to say, nothing. The butler turned out to be a friendly man, and the Rozenbergs remained in the Anna Vondelstraat. Even without them, the conditions in our house were precarious, with a baby a few weeks old, a little girl who was not yet toilet trained, eight adults (among whom for convenience I count my brother Jan's wife Fransje, who was a mere ten months older than I), and myself, a high school student without a school. The toilet's drainpipe froze and we had to use a metal waste barrel from the municipal garbage service. Each morning as early as possible after the curfew was lifted, my father took the barrel on an improvised cart to the Reynier Vinkeleskade and emptied it into the canal. Yet it seemed that the battle against hunger, filth, and shabbiness, which my parents so bravely fought, was being lost.

The Groenevelds, neighbours from across the street, came to the rescue. They were a kind, outgoing family with three children, two girls and a boy; the father was a dentist. The youngest child, the boy, was a student in the first grade of the school I had been attending. I sometimes helped him with his homework. When the electricity had been cut off, they discovered that the main cable still worked because it fed the Central Israelite Hospital, which had been "taken over" by the *Landwacht* (Landguard), a Dutch paramilitary Nazi organization. A simple operation enabled the Groenevelds to tap electricity, and every day they brought us an enormous pot with boiling hot water "to wash the babies." I think that pot of water saved my mother from sliding into despair.

There was fatalistic resignation in my parents' reaction when Germans entered our house for the second time. This happened in the first half of February, early in the evening; it was already dark and Dorus and Marja were upstairs in bed. Uncle and Aunt Bertha had barely managed to reach the deep closet in the living room. The trap door to the space under the floor was open, but they were afraid to lower themselves and close the trap door lest the noise would give them away. Everybody else was in the front room. It must have been a kind of *tableau vivant*: nobody moved; even the two Germans did not budge after having entered the room. After a while, one of them wandered somewhat hesitatingly to the living room. The other, who had caught a glance from my mother, muttered: *Was wir tun ist ekelhaft* (What we are doing is disgusting). Now she looked him straight in the eyes and asked: *Warum tun Sie es denn?* (Then, why do you do it?). Softly, his voice sounding almost friendly, he said: *Ich bin auch nicht so frei wie Sie denken* (Me too, I am not as free as you think). After this confession there was again an awkward silence. The German who had fumbled about in the living room without opening the closet door came back with a questioning expression on his face. His companion turned towards him and said, raising his voice, somewhat: *Schluss, wir hauen ab* (Enough, off we go). My father accompanied them to the front door. It almost seemed as if he was showing out guests. In the front hall he encountered a man who grabbed a stone jar from a stand, and with a loud "Goddamn" put it in an enormous burlap sack, after which he followed the Germans outside. Later we heard from the Groenevelds that two men with hats down over their eyes and carrying what looked like duffel bags had stood waiting near the front door.

That even a German had human feelings was reason for some hope. And when, towards the end of February, the drainage pipe of the toilets thawed without causing flooding, and the Swedish Red Cross distributed white bread and margarine, everybody took heart again. That the margarine was strictly vegetarian, as Aunt Bertha claimed, only Uncle believed, but we were glad they accepted their share. We even joked about white bread with peanut butter, for in the cellar on the shelf reserved for the Rozenbergs' supplies there actually was a jar of peanut butter. We sometimes went down to look at it; on the label it read: "peanut butter, inexpensive and tasty, also within your reach." In spite of arguments such as "a little bit doesn't matter" and "they probably don't even remember we have their peanut butter," my parents held firm. Once again they did not fall for remarks that were not entirely intended to be funny. Even without peanut butter we already felt half-liberated, because the Swedish bread seemed to have restored contact with the outside world. And yet we were not out of danger.

One springlike afternoon in early March, only my two brothers and our four Jewish refugees were home when there was a knock at the door. Aunt Bertha opened the little window in the front door and shut it again as fast as she could. A single police detective was standing there and ordered her to let him in. She alerted the men, let the children continue their afternoon sleep, put on her raincoat, and stepped outside. "I am going to call the police at a doctor's house nearby where there is a phone," she said, after having looked at the policeman's identification. "There are so many people who claim to be police," and off she went. My mother was the first to come home. She let in the detective, who turned out to be Sam Oly, a Dutch Nazi policeman who was notorious for hunting Jews, and on his order she showed him around the house. Furious, he followed her, cursing that impertinent Jewess who had slipped away from under his fingers. My mother did not react, but when, before Dorus's crib, he noted, "This is a Jew!" she asked, "What makes you say so?" Uncle Wiggerman and Jan had disappeared without a trace into the hiding place. However Kees, who had locked himself in my father's study, had to come out. At first he refused to unlock the door, but my mother persuaded him to do so. Because of the commotion outside the study, the room opposite it, where Marja had her nap, was overlooked. She did hear the noise, but contrary to her habit she did not call out when she woke up, and waited until she was lifted out of her bed.

Meanwhile, Sam Oly waited downstairs near the front door for my father and possibly other members of the family to come home. Nobody came home, however, because the Groenevelds' son had gone outside to play soccer with a friend as soon as his parents had noticed something was wrong. When the boys saw one of us approaching, they kicked the ball in our direction, and, while fetching it, warned: "Don't go home! Go to the dentist." Eventually Sam Oly left, leaving orders for my father to report to him the next morning before nine o'clock at the police station on Leidse Plein (Leiden Square).

When the coast was clear again and everyone was home except for Aunt Bertha, who had fled to Erna Kropveld as we had guessed, we quickly decided that all of us should go into hiding. The real fugitives and my father disappeared that same evening before curfew time; the rest of the family was going to leave the next morning. We packed the necessities, and when the children of the dentist and a boy who lived farther down the street came to offer their help, my mother also packed the table silver for them to take away. After the silver, a few paintings followed—everything was too good to leave for the Germans—and the mood became cheerful, as we were united by our loathing of the oppressor.

The next morning, all the helpers of the previous day showed up again. My sister Elisabeth's new friend, Bertus Willebrands, a tall man of few words whom she had met in the Resistance movement, had also come to help. In the heat of preparing to leave, we continued after nine o'clock; Sam Oly would definitely not come before ten. But at a quarter past nine I heard a loud warning cry: "Mrs. Schogt, here comes Mr. Oly!" My mother went to the front door, while all the other people fled through the garden gate towards safety. Again Sam Oly was alone. With my mother he went through the now-abandoned house where everything was in a mess. He ordered her to stay with him, while he watched at the front door for a passing member of the Dutch Nazi militia or a German soldier who could assist him. By chance nobody came, so there was no one to take his place when he went to the toilet. He left the door of the toilet open, but when my mother followed him, he shut it. She grabbed Aunt Bertha's fur coat from the coat stand and ran outside to the dentist's house, where we had been on the lookout, full of anxiety.

Our house was sealed, but because the Canadians had already cut off the lines of communication with Germany, its contents were not shipped east. When the war was over, everything was exactly as we had left it. The Jacobses had stayed in the vacated house of an aunt of my sister Elisabeth's friend; The aunt and her family had left Amsterdam because of the famine and had gone to the countryside to live. After the war the authorities immediately assigned a house to the Jacobs family. The son who had been hidden in Rotterdam was reunited with his parents. Later two daughters were born. Their ties with my parents remained very strong, even though they could no longer come for dinner, because of their strict religious ways. After Uncle had retired—he had once again become director of the Orthodox Jewish high school—the family emigrated to Jerusalem.

Marja's parents did not come back. That her father had perished in a concentration camp we already knew. The fact that her mother had been caught a few months after Marja had come to us, and that she probably had been sent on to Bergen-Belsen, had also somehow reached us during the war. The news that she had died there we heard after the Liberation. Her grandparents on her mother's side, who did survive in hiding, took Marja into their care. For all of us, the departure of Marja, who had brought so much joy during the second half of the war and of whom we were very fond, was a heavy blow. Her still fairly young grandparents had a lifestyle totally different from that of my parents. Although we maintained contact for some time, Marja almost entirely disappeared from our lives. Many years later she resumed the relationship, but as she said, it was too late. "I should have stayed with you," she once said to my sister. In 1970 Marja put an end to her life.

Mrs. Bloem came to visit in July 1945 to hear how everyone had fared. Only my sister, who was in bed with the flu, was home. When Mrs. Bloem inquired about "that darling little girl who stayed with you," my sister told her of the raids and the threat *das jüdische Kind mitzunehmen* (to take away the Jewish child). "How mean! How awful," Mrs. Bloem said. My sister added: "Yes, and what is most awful, we think that you denounced us." Mrs. Bloem turned very pale, started to tremble, and stuttered: "I did not mean to." Then she got up and quickly left. We never saw her again.

Freddie did not come back. The Rozenbergs moved again to their house in the Johannes Verhulststraat, perhaps the only Jewish house that had never been raided. Mr. Rozenberg's health deteriorated, and he died a few years after Liberation. I do not know whether he smoked all the cigars that had not fallen into the hands of the Germans.

In the Dark
1940-55

THERE ARE PEOPLE who neatly order and file away all the letters they receive. When, after their death, relatives or friends clean up, they find bundles of mail with the name of the writer and sometimes the years when the correspondence took place. Nobody knows what to do: after all the care the deceased took in storing the letters it would be rude and insensitive to throw them away. If—as usually happens—nobody can be found willing to take charge of the whole collection, the only solution is to return the letters and postcards to their senders, if they are still alive.

Rereading one's own letters written a long time ago, full of clumsy passages and repetition, is never a totally pleasant experience, but usually the vivid images of the past that are evoked provide ample compensation. However, when I received a small package of mail I had sent over the years to my Aunt Grie, who had just died, there was no such satisfaction. The package contained Christmas and New Year's greetings with pictures of our children, and a few birthday letters. I felt confused and embarrassed, and was amazed that she had kept the letters, wondering if there had not been hidden motives at play when I wrote those blandly kind messages. But I did not throw out those letters; that task remains for the next generation.

Aunt Grie was my mother's younger sister, the third child born to my grandparents. The first, a boy, died in infancy. My grandfather worked as a graphic designer at the Van Houten's chocolate factory at Weesp, about fifteen kilometres east of Amsterdam. When the girls reached high school age—my aunt was about two years younger than my mother—the family moved to Amsterdam, where both grandparents had grown up. It was cheaper for my grandfather to commute to Weesp than to send his daughters to school every day in Amsterdam. From the stories I heard about him, he emerges as a hardworking, extremely thrifty man who laid down the law in his family. My grandmother, a gentle woman not without a certain sense of humour, must undoubtedly have suffered under his tyrannical reign. Apparently she had severe bouts of envy. Later in life this affliction diminished, and I remember only one incident. After the family that lived above them had said goodbye before going to spend a week somewhere in a wooded part of the country, my grandmother walked around sulking for half a day. Then, all of a sudden, she stated, "I am jealous," and in doing so, dispelled her mood.

The two van Rijn sisters did not have a cheerful youth, but that fact did not foster a feeling of solidarity. Or maybe it did, for even when I thought that my parents should cut ties with Grie, my mother continued the relationship of armed peace and acrimony: "She is my only sister, and there it is." They were both intelligent; both had gone to university, but it had not been easy. After completing modern high school, my mother had spent a year earning money by tutoring high school students, all the while studying Greek and Latin in preparation for the state examinations in these languages, for in those days knowledge of the classical languages was considered indispensable for university entrance. To celebrate her success in the exams, a small evening party was organized to which her two best friends from high school had been invited as well as the father of one of them, a friendly man who sometimes, on his days off, went on a bicycle tour with the girls. No doubt small pastries and fine assorted butter cookies were passed around, and maybe they even drank to my mother's future before my grandfather made a short speech. He said he was proud of his eldest daughter, who had shown she deserved the support of her parents. Of course she would continue living at home, but as an adult she would have to share in the upkeep of the household. That night my mother cried before she fell asleep.

She studied mathematics, against the wishes of her father who had wanted her to become a pharmacist, a profession he thought would be lucrative. When she was in university she got to know my father, a quiet, introverted math student, and again my grandfather disapproved. He was so angry about their eventual marriage that he refused for many years to cross their threshold, and a reconciliation only occurred after their third child was named after him: Jan Carel Marinus.

No matter how unenviable my mother's circumstances had been, Grie understandably felt even more disadvantaged. She was not allowed to study a year for her state exams in Greek and Latin, but had to look for a job right after high school. After working in an office in Amsterdam for a few years, she took the exams all the same, passed them, and studied law. ("I was able to take part in all sorts of student activities and had a much better time than your mother.") She received her Ph.D. on *stellingen*, at the time an easier, less prestigious dissertation consisting of a number of small theses. ("Yes, Grie has her degree," my mother used to say, "but she did not have to write a real dissertation; things were very easy for law students at the time.") From then on she was Master Doctor Greta W. van Rijn, even though her real name was Grietje Wigles. Her initials G.W. had aroused my mother's envy when they were children because on the feast of Saint Nicholas, when chocolate initials were given, Grie's chocolate letters were much bigger than the I and J of Ida Jacoba. Today, all the letters of the alphabet have the same weight. That was a long time ago, however, and I never discovered traces of jealousy behind my mother's almost constant irritation with her sister. She could not help pricking what she thought was Grie's balloon of ostentatious self-complacency, and boasting each time she had an opportunity to do so. I remember one day when Grie, flattening her then already bulging stomach, and with rouge on her cheeks, asked my mother, who was busy cooking, "Don't you think I look healthy?" My mother half turned around, examined her sister with a sharp, critical, and disapproving look, and slowly said: "Yes…if it is real…."

Grie's entire life was marked by the opposition between genuine and false, and many of her deeds and actions were provocative. She joined activist groups and immediately volunteered to be a propagandist and, as it were, fully identified with her new colleagues. Her first job after she finished her studies was in Zeeland. Later, Grie occasionally introduced a statement by saying, "We in Zeeland," or "As we in Zeeland say," although she had left Zeeland years before. She lived in Brussels for many years. There, possibly in the early thirties, she joined the Flemish movement and became a Roman Catholic. My father, who seldom commented on his sister-in-law's decisions, and who was, in matters of faith, a very tolerant atheist, said being born a Catholic was understandable, but that one had to be *meshugge* (crazy) to become one. My mother, who, like her own mother, belonged to the Dutch Mennonite congregation, which is much more liberal than much of its Canadian counterpart, fully agreed with him, even though she would have chosen different words. For a while Grie's Dutch was loaded with French words, a speech habit that was difficult to reconcile with the Flemish movement, but fitted nicely with the *femme du monde* image to which she aspired. Once, holidaying with us on the island of Texel, she asked for *papier gommé* in a little shop that sold beach equipment, candy, and stationery. No, that they did not have. My brother Jan came to the rescue and asked if there was gummed paper. Yes, fortunately there was.

Not only her French attracted attention. Her clothes, too, were out of the ordinary, ranging from cheap-looking shiny chic to shoddy dresses of flowery material that clashed with her red hair and worn out, faded sweaters. But it was mainly her loud, emphatic, lecturing voice and her shrill, sometimes cackling laugh that made people look at her with amazed amusement. After the death of my elder sister Ynske, my other sister Elisabeth and I stayed with her in The Hague where, after her Brussels years, she had found a job as secretary (not uncommon, during the economic depression, despite her law degree) in a small metal business. She gave us, whenever we took a streetcar, a guided tour. She told us many interesting facts about the buildings we passed, addressing all the other passengers as well. In a restaurant, she once grabbed a french fry from my plate, dipped it in mustard and declared, triumphantly looking around the filled dining hall, "That's how we in Belgium eat fries!" Often, in such situations, she engaged in lively conversations with total strangers, which meant that we could stay in the background.

Apart from a few awkward moments, among them my almost fainting in the Catholic church ("You just do everything like me," she had told us) and the hurried retreat to the fresh air outside, the days spent in The Hague were a great success. Grie rented two rooms in a nondescript house in a nondescript street near the Juliana van Stolberglaan, but she managed to make us feel at home. Sleeping was makeshift, and one evening she said, with a coquettish smile, "The little one"—that is what she used to call me—"is really too old to see a lady in her slip." I was ten years old and not particularly interested in aunts in shiny pink rayon.

Aunt Grie never married. I do not know if she had lovers. In a small, brownish photograph from her Belgian period one can vaguely recognize her, young and slim, with the kind of hat that only the Queen of England wears nowadays. With her is a short gentleman in a tailored coat, holding a bowler hat in his hand. His name was Fons, but nothing came of it. There was a relationship with Herbert, when she was already over forty and lived in her own house in the Laan van Nieuw Oost Indië in The Hague. Like her father, she was forever wheeling and dealing in shares and bonds; apparently she was good at it, for as a secretary she would not have earned enough to buy a house. Nobody in the family ever saw Herbert, and it is highly unlikely that he spent a single night in her house, or even had dinner there. Yet, the general reaction was one of strong disapproval and indignation, although I must confess that I was also curious, and would have liked to have met him.

We heard about him for the first time at a family reunion on my grandparents' golden wedding anniversary in the summer of 1940. They had decided against a big celebration with speeches and skits by the grandchildren and a real dinner in a hotel; because of the German invasion, the destruction of Rotterdam, and the capitulation, the mood was sombre. Only tea was served, and we, the children, each received twenty guilders to spend in whatever way we wanted. Grie, who had been in Amsterdam shortly before, could not make it on the day itself. After a remark by my mother that it was a pity Grie was absent—in those times one especially felt the need to be with family and friends— the golden anniversary groom, who did not feel very festive anyway, burst out: "Oh, Grie, let her stay in The Hague with her German!" Grie with a German? Grie, who always raved about the royal family—when she showed us the palace, Het Huis ten Bosch, it seemed as if she personally knew all the members of the House of Orange and was their friend—Grie with a Kraut? This was unthinkable! Grandfather must be mistaken, he must have misunderstood her.

When she visited Amsterdam again a month later, it became apparent that he had understood her perfectly. When a German had asked her the way, she had somehow been drawn into a conversation with him. She had started by saying that "her" The Hague was a Dutch city, a remark that seemed to us rather superfluous. The German had said that he knew that already and that he had come in order to help the Dutch solve their problems. "Such a nice boy, his name is Herbert and he lives in Cologne. I sent an Edam cheese to his mother. She has a hard time now that her son in the army is so far away." Grie even showed a picture from some German journal, of two German soldiers on a motorbike with a sidecar. "The one on the driver's seat is Herbert; he gave me the picture before he left for France." "One cannot see anything in that picture; they could be anybody with those stupid helmets on and seen from behind," Elisabeth said. "Is he coming back to Holland?" I asked, for I would have liked to get to know a German better. "Well, I hope he never comes back, he does not belong here, let him go to his mother in Cologne," my sister commented. My parents had a faint smile, and Aunt Grie began to breathe heavily, in her case an unmistakable sign of being indignant and hurt.

Herbert disappeared from her life, for nothing came of his promise of letters. Moreover, at their last meeting in Voorburg they had almost quarrelled when Grie had reminded him of his Sabbath duties. He replied ("I was so upset when I heard it," she commented) that he did not give a damn for a Jew who had gone and hanged himself on a cross to deceive the world. Almost immediately after this shocking bit of information, her tone became sentimental: "He called me Gretchen." My mother thought that the whole affair had little to do with pro-German sentiments, but a lot with the fact that her sister was a spinster over forty-five by then. This also explained why she felt such an urge to speak about it to an audience that was anything but receptive. My father made no comment, which probably meant that he had his own thoughts about the behaviour of his sister-in-law.

Fairly soon after the Herbert episode, she changed jobs, leaving no room for doubt about her pro-German inclinations: she became the secretary of the Pharmacists' Chamber, an institution, as she explained, that looked after pharmacies that had been "taken over." Later she also talked about "the businesses whose owners have left." Each time she used one of these veiled Nazi terms, she was corrected by one of us: not "left" but "deported," not "taken over" but "stolen." Of course she persisted in her jargon, and twisted everything so that black became white, and white, black. One day—it must have been in the spring of 1942, because after the mass deportations began in July of that year I refused to go out with her—near the Rijksmuseum, a German soldier asked us the way to the Leidse plein. I pointed the wrong way. When he was already at a considerable distance, Aunt Grie was puzzled: "But the Leidse plein is not in that direction, is it?" "I know," I proudly declared. Her reaction was swift: "This is typically Amsterdam. In The Hague we are used to foreigners and help them."

She thought we had become cheeky, yet she continued to visit us. Just before all students were ordered to sign a declaration of loyalty to the German authorities in the winter of 1943 and the universities were closed because hardly anybody signed, my brother Jan and a few friends played with their jazz band in a café in Gouda. Grie went there by bike one afternoon to listen. She wrote afterwards to my parents that this weird music in a hole filled with smoke was utterly decadent. On her way back to The Hague she came across a group of "Little Gulls" of the National Socialist Youth Brigade, who were singing old Dutch songs. What a contrast! She never became a member of the Dutch National Socialist League, and at least that much can be said in her favour. But, then, this may have been sheer calculation on her part.

The longer the war lasted the less frequent the contact between the two sisters became. During her rare visits the Jacobses who had come to live with us in the late fall of 1943, stayed away, although my parents did not think Grie would denounce them. This was not much of a problem because Grie always stayed with my grandparents when in Amsterdam, and used to announce her visits to us in writing or by phone. She did see Marja, the little girl whom my parents had taken into their house as a baby about six months before the Jacobses came. My sister told her a fantastic story about a Hungarian friend who had had to return quickly to Budapest with her husband, where she had become seriously ill, and her plan to come back for Marja had fallen through; now it was probably wiser to wait until the end of the war because travel had become so dangerous. "But when she returns to Budapest she will speak Hungarian, and I won't be able to understand her any more," my sister Elisabeth concluded in a sad voice. Grie's comment was: "As soon as I saw her I thought she was not Dutch, but looked Hungarian." With this not quite believable evidence of ethnic insight, Marja was, as it were, legalized, to everyone's great relief.

Running a household was not easy in the last winter of the war. It would have helped to know for sure that it was the last winter, but even so it would have been difficult to cope without gas or electricity, without heat and with steadily shrinking, completely insufficient rations. My parents bravely tried to make the best of it, even when the Jacobses became parents of a little boy, and even when my brother Jan "had to get married," as people used to say in those days. Somehow the announcement of the wedding had been sent to The Hague. It was a reassuring thought that the message would probably never reach its destination, and that even if Grie received it, she would not be able to come because of the general railway strike and the discontinuation of bus service. "At least that's one complication we won't have," my father said, and my mother did not say that she would miss her only sister.

On 28 December, at half past eleven in the morning, Grie knocked at the front door, three weeks after Dorus Jacobs was born, and a week before Jan's wedding. Everybody was in the room where my mother cooked on an emergency stove and where it was slightly less cold. Thus Grie, who barged in, brushing aside whoever had opened the door, happened to find Mr. and Mrs. Jacobs. My father, who always thought much while saying little and was always prepared for the worst, introduced them to Grie: "Mr. and Mrs. Wiggerman, refugees from Arnhem, temporarily billeted with us." She barely seemed to listen. She sank down on a chair and immediately began to tell how she had come on foot from The Hague. She had spent the night at cousin Kitty's in Vogelenzang, and nice soldiers had given her a ride from Haarlem to Amsterdam. Her baggage consisted of a backpack and a small suitcase that later turned out to contain a portable typewriter, but she was not thirty any more, and she was very tired from lugging this load. Kept in check by our parents' hidden signals, we limited our reaction to a whispered: "Nice soldiers? Awful Krauts! Not thirty any more? Fifty!"

Grie's short visit—unfortunately she could not stay until the wedding, for she had to be back at work after New Year's day—created a mood of almost cheerful solidarity, and provided entertainment in tense moments. After she had eaten something and recovered from her exhausting expedition, she started a conversation at once with Aunt Bertha, alias Mrs. Wiggerman. "What was it like for you being in Arnhem and expecting the little boy, and how did you end up in Amsterdam?" There was an anxious silence. As a group leader of the Dutch Travel Association, Grie had been everywhere and seemed to be knowledgeable even about places where she had never set foot. Aunt Bertha closed her eyes and said, with restrained emotion, "Everything was so terrible. I'd rather not talk about it." With a trace of disappointment, but also full of understanding, Grie accepted the answer that left room for imagining the most gruesome events. The lie about Arnhem was almost discovered only one other time. As always, when someone had to go to a distant destination in the city, a lively discussion took place about the shortest route there. Grie persisted in emphatically defending her route against my brother Jan, who did not give an inch either. All of a sudden, Uncle Wiggerman entered the debate. He had been listening to Grie with mounting irritation and he could not contain himself any longer: "Of course Jan is right, it is much quicker when one takes the Constantijn Huyghensstraat and the de Clercqstraat before...." "People from Arnhem don't know such things," whispered my mother, who was standing behind him, and he stopped in mid-sentence.

There were no more dangerous moments, but one constantly felt tension in the air, and every so often verbal skirmishes broke out. When Grie told us that Mr. Grendel, her boss, had managed to keep the office open, while most enterprises in The Hague had been closed for lack of heating, our reaction was: "Big deal for a Nazi who works for the Germans." When Grie looked for a place to do the typing she had brought with her—even during the day our house was very dark, and there was only enough light near the windows for reading—we made room for her reluctantly and under protest. Yet nobody would have liked to miss the sight of Grie in front of her typewriter in the fading December light. She looked as if she was going to launch an attack. With her upper lip tightly pulled over her teeth and her lower lip jutting forward and curled down, she went on the offensive. I can still see her typing with two fingers, each time raising her hands high above the keyboard. In spite of this strange style she developed remarkable speed, yet made little progress with her work. In the bustle of the only more or less heated room, where diapers were constantly hung for drying and interest in the preparation of meals was inversely proportional to the quantity of food available, she could not concentrate. Only in the evening did things quiet down, but then there was rarely any light.

My sister Elisabeth had been given an acetylene lamp, for which the Resistance movement provided carbide once in a while when she had a lot of work to do. As a member of the editorial staff of a left-wing news bulletin, involved in finding houses where Jews could hide and in the distribution of illegal ration coupons, she could sometimes barely cope. On the third evening of Grie's visit, unexpectedly as always, she gave the signal for an evening of reading: "There is so much to do, we should light the lamp, I think." Everybody reacted immediately by fetching either a book or some work for which good light was needed. People settled around the lamp, which when placed on the middle of the table spread a white, almost blinding light. Grie, of course unfamiliar with the carbide ritual, had watched the sudden outburst of activity with amazement, but when she understood what it was all about, she quickly disappeared to her bedroom. A moment later she returned with her typewriter and a folder with papers and explained rather superfluously, "I must still finish a report." Elisabeth, who had been looking for various papers, was the last to come back into the room. She took in the situation at a glance and exclaimed: "What! My underground carbide for those Nazi reports!" and blew out the lamp. I do not remember exactly what we did during the rest of the evening in the dark, but it turned out to be one of the cosiest we had during the famine winter, without Grie, who had retired, breathing heavily.

She left according to plan the next morning, while all of us watched, feeling relieved, yet a little guilty. It was her last visit to us during the war. Her house in the Laan van Nieuw Oost Indië remained standing in a zone of destruction when the Allied forces bombed the Bezuidenhout area in The Hague. The only damage was a crack in the foundation, and after the war she received parcels from a relief committee of American University Women as a victim of war. I do not know whether she tried also to get compensation from the Dutch government. Maybe she thought it wiser not to draw too much attention to herself, although that is not very likely in view of what happened shortly after Liberation.

In April, my maternal grandmother had died, quietly extinguished, wasted away, although it was not clear whether one could count her among the victims of the famine. In February, my mother had tried to persuade her parents to move in with us, telling them on that occasion about the people who were in hiding. My grandfather then replied that he was responsible for the safety of his wife and that "those people" should leave: "Let the Jews look after themselves." So they did not come, and all sorts of complications were avoided, but it also meant that the weekly expeditions to visit them in the Alexanderkade, one hour on foot each way, had to continue.

Soon after Liberation, Grie appeared again in Amsterdam. Nice soldiers had given her a ride part way. She stayed on to look after my grandfather, who could perfectly manage without her, and with whom she bickered continuously. She did not even mention The Hague, which made us think that she was keeping a low profile for safety. One afternoon in June, the bell rang and we found a blonde girl standing at our front door. She looked upset and, once inside, immediately began to speak in a plaintive voice, without introducing herself. Something horrible had happened; Miss van Rijn had been arrested; they locked her up. "Life is so precarious and unsafe these days," she said. My mother remarked that, on the contrary, we were enjoying much greater safety and stability now that the Germans had left. Then she asked what precisely had happened. At the trial of her father—"I am Trudie Grendel"—Miss van Rijn was in the public gallery when…She took a newspaper clipping from her purse, saying "It was in the paper this morning."

> Yesterday afternoon, during the trial of Mr. G., former head of the Pharmacists' Chamber, there was some commotion in the public gallery

when some of those who were present recognized Miss G. v. R., his secretary. She was arrested and led away.

After Trudie—or was her name Truus?—had left, my parents went to the Alexanderkade. They were told by my grandfather that three days before Grie had been visited by an acquaintance from The Hague. The next day she had left for that city, saying that she must make some arrangements there.

Two days later an official notice arrived that she had been interned in a detention centre at the Goudse Singel in Rotterdam. She was allowed to receive one parcel and one letter twice a week. After three weeks they let her go. She was deeply indignant about the scandalous treatment in "the camp," where ladies were ordered to clean "the privies." Comparisons with other camps were never made, and she was not affected by what came to light afterwards about the concentration camps of the Third Reich. During the first years after the war, the topics of persecution and of the suffering of the victims of the Nazis receded to the background and, slowly, relations with Grie were restored, although an undercurrent of genuinely negative feelings had been added to our prewar irritation.

That undercurrent surfaced again when I was about to marry a Jewish girl. The few times Grie met Corrie, she stayed as distant as possible when shaking hands, and never called her by her first name. A few weeks before our wedding, Grie happened to be present when several parcels were delivered for us at my parents' house. She looked disapprovingly at the labels on the boxes, saying, "Of course! The Bijenkorf and Gerzon, only Jewish stores!" At that moment, my parents should have shown her the door and cut all ties with her, I thought, but nothing happened and I did not do anything either.

Grie did not attend the reception in the home of my sister-in-law and her husband on 2 April 1955, after the official wedding ceremony at City Hall in Amsterdam. It was during Holy Week, and, according to her, it was highly improper to have festivities then. She was living in Breda, surrounded by kindred spirits as far as politics and religion were concerned. After my grandfather's death, she had left Amsterdam again and chosen "Brabant's little The Hague," as Breda was called, rather than returning to The Hague itself. Corrie and I rarely saw her, and after we emigrated to Canada, contact was limited to a few birthday letters and New Year's wishes. I hope I wrote to her because I thought she was, after all, a somewhat pathetic, lonely old woman, and my mother's only sister.

She did not disinherit us, although according to my brother Jan, who had kept in touch with her and was the executor of her will, the idea had more than once crossed her mind. Grie's money was used to pay for the university years in Amsterdam of our son, the son of a Jewish mother.

Mussels
1936-42

It was one of those balmy Toronto nights we always long for during the winter. We were walking home after a very congenial evening with friends who had prepared an elaborate and refined meal. I had particularly enjoyed the mussels in a white wine sauce because it meant for me that I had finally grown up. When I was a child, I thoroughly detested fish and seafood, and that always elicited the comment that I was just like my father. Much later, in situations where saying that I disliked fish was more difficult than trying to eat it, I began to get used to it, although my children and Corrie, my wife, said that I looked like a condemned prisoner rather than someone enjoying his meal. Even that aspect of the struggle with the inhabitants of the sea changed, and on this particular evening I had genuinely liked what I ate. It gave me a childish feeling of triumph so that I remarked, "Don't you think it's marvellous that I can now eat mussels and enjoy them?" "Yes, and even I have overcome my aversion," Corrie said quietly. And suddenly the war was there again, the war about which my oldest daughter, once asked by a friend whether we talked about it too little or too much, had answered, "Neither, but it was always there."

I felt ashamed that I did not remember the evening Corrie had mentioned once or twice before, when her family was having mussels for dinner, on 19 December 1942. I tried to visualize what had happened, how her father had come home late and found the rest of the family already at the table. But, as always, I did not succeed in getting a clear picture, because vital details were missing.

I never knew my parents-in-law; they died about ten years before I came into the Frenkel family. As time went by, I was able to piece together more or less what they were like from what my sisters-in-law, my wife, and other relatives told me about them. There are many pictures in photo albums, small black and white, somewhat yellowed snapshots taken in the garden or on holiday outings. Happy, smiling people in sunny surroundings, family gatherings with several rows of relatives looking towards the camera—but these do not tell very much about what went on in their minds. There is also a portrait of my father-in-law by a not widely known but gifted painter, whom he had helped with legal matters. The painting hangs in the house that Corrie's father built in 1929, and where my oldest sister-in-law and her husband are still living. Every time we visit them, I look at the portrait and try to discover what is behind that serious, almost stern expression, so different from the one seen in the photo albums.

My mother-in-law, of whom there is no painting, had a rather serious, almost worried look even when she was smiling in the photos. I would like to have talked with her and found out what worried her, but when I imagine a conversation with her, I realize that an essential element is missing: I do not know what her voice—or his for that matter—was like. I can, however, easily guess what preoccupied her. Apart from the inevitable worries of having a family with children, there were portentous clouds on the political horizon and the great Depression of the thirties brought many reasons for concern.

Their start in life must have been quite happy. Corrie's father grew up in Utrecht, the middle child of three. His father was an antique dealer. He and his older brother were the first generation to go to university, he taking law, his brother, medicine. Philip, or as it is shortened in Dutch, Flip, was a brilliant student, who even wrote a full-fledged Ph.D. dissertation, although in those days one could obtain a doctor's degree in law in a shorter and much easier way, like my Aunt Grie had done. He actively took part in student life, was a member of a fraternity (when, much later, I was a student, I disliked fraternities as bastions of class elitism) and, being small and light, was the coxswain of a four at the yearly student regattas. For him it was undoubtedly a good feeling to be accepted and to do well in this student world. During World War I, while he was doing his military service at a fortress near Utrecht that went back to Roman times, he dug up some small antique vases.

The parents Frenkel with their children from left to right: Tilie, Tineke, Corrie. Bentveld, 1929.

They were the beginning of a collection that is still kept in a glass display case, placed against the dining room window overlooking the garden.

Corrie's mother spent her early years in Middelburg, the small capital town of the province of Zeeland in the southwest of the country. Her father and his brother had a store in the centre of the town, where they sold textiles. She went to the local gymnasium and wanted to study medicine. In a picture taken during a bicycle trip with a group of girl-friends and classmates, she is the only one wearing pants instead of the impractical long skirts that were the required outfit for young ladies in those days. Although they looked older, the girls must have been just seventeen or eighteen. Betsy Adèle Wiener, whom her family and friends called Bep, was apparently rather unconventional. Many years later she decided to get a licence to drive trucks and buses in case the country needed her. Even her choice of studying medicine at Utrecht University was uncommon for a girl and was a sign of her independence of mind.

This independence was not strong enough for her to continue her studies after her marriage, shortly after the end of World War 1. Flip's brother and Bep's sister had not waited till the war was over; their wedding took place in 1916. I always talk about my wife's cousins as "double cousins," although I do not know if that expression is standard English.

Flip was born in 1889 and Bep in 1898, so there was a considerable difference in age, which is not apparent in their photos. My own impression is that she was more inclined to worry, less optimistic than he. Their three daughters have different memories of their parents, partly because they are very different themselves in spite of striking similarities, partly because they were different ages at the moment of separation. As memory is selective, their own later lives have also undoubtedly coloured their reactions. The oldest sister, Tilie, thinks that behind her mother's seriousness and the hint of sadness there lay deep frustration at not having continued university. Tilie, as well as the second sister, Tineke, both completed their medical studies after they were married, and combined medical work and family life. Tineke was, until recently, rather reticent to talk about the war years, and I rarely spoke to her about her parents, but once she surprised me by commenting, when looking at a photograph, "That smile of hers in this picture has always bothered me." I realized that it was, indeed, a vague smile; I felt it was one more sign of her fight against intrinsic sadness. This may well be a retrospective interpretation on my part, because it fits so well with what happened to the family in later years.

Their start after they were married was anything but sad. Flip became a partner in a well-established law firm in Amsterdam. They rented an upstairs apartment in the neighbourhood of the Concertgebouw, in a quiet, residential middle- or upper-middle-class quarter of town. The three daughters were born in 1921, 1924, and 1927. The last to come was perhaps a little disappointment for the father, who would have liked to have a son and sometimes called her "Cornelis," a boy's name, instead of Corrie, as she was officially called. That in itself was quite an achievement, because in those days children could be registered only under an acknowledged name, and fantasy names and abbreviations such as "Corrie" were not allowed. His persuasive skills as a lawyer were stronger than the law. Corrie was named after her aunt, whom everybody called Cor, although her full name was Carolina Selina. About fifteen years later her father would again successfully plead his case when much more than a first name was at stake.

The good fortunes of the young family continued, and in the late twenties Flip and Bep had a house built in a wooded area west of Haarlem, near the dunes and a short drive from the beach at Zandvoort. They moved to their new house in 1929, pioneers of the army of well-to-do city dwellers who settled in the countryside. The house has changed little, if at all, and even now, almost seventy years later, it is striking, more by its welcoming, hospitable features than by its size. It had a large garden, with a little pond, shrubs, and flowers. There was a road bordered on both sides by majestic oak trees, and beyond that unspoilt forests ideal for walking and playing, although children had to be warned about solitary strangers. The area is completely developed now, and has become an affluent residential area. But just as my father-in-law did in the early days, many inhabitants still commute to Amsterdam. Flip went every morning to the railway station on his bicycle, a fifteen-minute ride, took the train to Amsterdam, and walked to his office. On the way back home he always paid a short visit to his mother, who lived halfway between his house and the station. She originally came from Würzburg in Germany, and had maintained a fairly strong German accent. It is quite possible that Bep did not altogether like these stopovers and would have preferred her husband to come straight home. Yet he seemed to be totally successful: a lawyer, a devoted son, husband, and father.

Corrie remembers him full of life and jokes, "But Flip!" often being the indulgent comment of her mother. But he was also a great help to his daughters, reading Latin and the Old Testament with Tilie, and encouraging Corrie to go to the gymnasium, although the two older sisters believed she was not serious enough for such a difficult school, and should be sent to an easier one.

Although the stock exchange on Wall Street crashed, and the Great Depression began soon after the family moved to their new house, there is no reference to financial problems when the three sisters remember their growing up in Bentveld. On the contrary, the oldest of the three remembers that she felt embarrassed about her privileged situation.

Of course no family goes through life without problems. The middle sister, Tineke, had weak legs, and Bep went with her to a world-famous specialist in Germany when that country was not the most pleasant place to visit. Tineke was treated, and then had to wear soft leather leggings for more than a year. From then on she was able to take part in strenuous walks and even hikes in the mountains. Less serious, yet sadder because of its end, was the story of Corrie's pet white rabbit. On a warm day when the snow was melting, she put the animal on a layer of straw outside, thinking that it needed fresh air. The rabbit caught a cold and died of pneumonia soon afterwards. Apart from facing such major and minor worries, the family was a happy one. Corrie fondly remembers the Friday night dinners at her grandmother's house, visits by car to Amsterdam once a year, and the snug, protected feeling when they drove home in the dark while she was half asleep. She remembers, too, the festive Saturdays when her father did not go to his office in Amsterdam, having again been an innovator, this time by introducing the five-day work week.

Yet they were not quite like the other families in the neighbourhood, who were, at most, only slightly alarmed by what was happening in Germany, or paid no attention to it at all. Right from the moment the Nazis came to power, Flip and Bep were deeply concerned, and, in the years that followed, a constant stream of refugees from Germany found temporary shelter in their house. One of them, a very handsome, athletically built young teacher of physical education, Ernst Hirsch, organized morning gym classes in the central hall on the first floor for the women, who came down in their underwear to take part in what was a welcome distraction. Corrie had a little girl's crush on him and loved to watch him exercising, or playing tennis. For Bep, however, the continuous stream of refugees was at times rather stressful.

I imagine that the men were often away, trying to arrange financial matters, looking for a more permanent residence, or applying for a permit to settle in the United States or somewhere else far from Germany. Flip, for his part, went on several occasions to Germany, smuggling valuables for the refugees on his way back to Holland. Once he was searched and frisked in the train near Cologne. In order to "help" the German police, he took off his coat—in which precious stones were hidden—and nothing was found. Maybe the story became more exciting each time it was repeated, but certainly life was not dull for Flip. Bep, however, had to deal with the drudgery of household chores and with guests who were displaced and unhappy, tending to idealize their past in Germany compared to their present in the Netherlands. The wives, who had little to do other than wait passively for things to work out, longed for the food they were used to back home, and seemed critical and ungrateful. Bep could not stand the attitude of *bei uns ist alles besser* (in our country everything is better), and began to dislike all Germans, non-Jews and Jews alike. That Tilie's boyfriend, Herbert Rothbarth, was a German refugee was not a point in his favour in Bep's eyes, whereas Flip, whose mother had come from Germany and who did not generalize, liked him very much and appreciated his quick and inquisitive mind. I am sure Bep would have come around to Flip's opinion in the long run, had things worked out differently.

The Friday-night dinners at grandmother's house were part of the Jewish custom, as was the hospitality and assistance given to Jewish refugees, but for the rest there was little that linked the family to the Jewish faith and traditions. Flip did not want a Christmas tree in his house, yet one year Tilie had secretly put a little one in her room in an act that was a mixture of teenage rebellion and the desire to be just like everybody else. In pre-war Holland, being like everyone else seemed almost possible, yet there were, even for Corrie, who was too young to be aware of what was going on in the world, moments when it was brought home to her that she was different. One year, when her whole class was going to make Christmas decorations out of red and green cardboard and tinsel, the well-meaning teacher discreetly whispered in her ear, "Of course you don't have to take part." On another occasion, when she was being difficult and whining, she overheard her nanny saying to the kitchen help, "Jews always spoil their children." She felt ashamed and stopped whining, but the temporary improvement of behaviour probably did not change the opinion of the two women. And then there was the Roman Catholic family on their street that did not allow their children to play with Jews. Fortunately, they were an exception, and although Corrie registered their attitude, she did not suffer very much from it, finding it rather strange and incomprehensible.

First and foremost feeling Dutch, leading the life of a well-to-do Dutch family, sustained by Flip's energetic optimism and held together by Bep's caring way of running the household, the family provided Corrie with a warm and sheltered childhood. As the youngest of the three sisters, she was sometimes taken along on family trips that were more to her sisters' and her parents' taste than to hers. As a result, a wonderful vacation trip to France and Switzerland in 1938 has left her with mixed memories. A girl taken along to look after her when the others went on mountain hikes, deemed too strenuous for the little one, suffered from dizziness and nausea because of high altitudes and was not very good company. Corrie was not altogether happy, but over the years the trip became a highlight of her memories, the last carefree major family outing.

The next summer they rented a cottage in the dunes of Terschelling, one of the Frisian islands, but the threat of war must have cast a shadow over that vacation. When the Germans invaded Poland, and what had been a threat became a reality, the last summer guests rushed home. The Netherlands remained neutral, just as in World War I. The army was vigilant, plans to inundate parts of the country in case of attack were ready—water had always been a reliable ally in such circumstances—and there were no signs of any shortage of food or energy. It was a fool's paradise, and people went on with their business, as if nothing was the matter, or so it seemed. Tilie went to the University of Utrecht in September to study medicine. She took part in student activities, made friends, and worked very hard. She and her best friend, Marietje, who was going to play a very important role a few years later and with whom Tilie has always remained very close, were rather frugal in their tastes. When Flip visited his oldest daughter he brought her the biggest box of Droste chocolates one could buy. It was a generous gesture of fatherly love, but also a personal statement in the battle of the generations over different lifestyles, for the girls, particularly Tilie, were embarrassed by their parents' affluence. Tineke continued, in the meantime, at the classical high school in Haarlem; Corrie was in the highest elementary school grade, hoping to join Tineke the year after.

Then on 10 May 1940, a beautiful sunny spring day as all history books and memoirs never forget to mention, the Germans invaded the Netherlands, attacking when it was still dark. When Corrie and her father, stunned and disconcerted, watched how a few Dutch aeroplanes were giving battle to what seemed a squadron of German fighters, she overheard him mutter softly, "This means the end for us."

Yet towards the end of the five-day war, when a relative, Uncle Max van der Veen, who lived close by, arrived in a hurry to ask whether Flip and Bep and their daughters wanted to join him and his family in fleeing to England, they declined the offer after agonizing deliberations, although realizing how extraordinary the offer was. About twenty years later, when Corrie and I were still in Amsterdam, one of the van der Veen daughters, Elly, and her husband, a liberal rabbi whose American English we had trouble understanding, came to visit us. They were very friendly, but somehow the reunion was awkward, and no one spoke of the visit of Uncle Max, Elly's father, though his pivotal offer was on everyone's mind. When we were in Princeton a few years later, we did not try to get in touch with them. We never saw Elly and her husband again.

What made Flip and Bep ultimately decide to stay in Holland we shall never know. Of course, the crossing of the North Sea in a small boat was risky while the war was raging, and the Germans had absolute supremacy in the air. And then there was Flip's mother, old and too frail to take part in the dangerous adventure. Could they possibly leave her behind alone and unprotected? Bep herself was not in the best of health either. The heavy task of running what could be called a transit shelter for many refugees, combined with the normal duties of a housewife and mother, had taken its toll. Bep was agitated, hyperactive, and yet always tired. She was definitely not in any condition to make crucial decisions about the future in a foreign country. As for Flip, he was probably not ready either to leave his law practice and the house he was so proud of in exchange for an existence in which he would have to start all over again and perhaps go door to door as a salesman of buttons or matches. So they stayed in Holland, the country they felt loyal to and loved. Like many others, Flip tried to reassure himself, thinking that the Germans would not and could not do to Dutch citizens what they were doing to the German Jews.

On 14 May 1940 the Germans bombed Rotterdam, destroying its centre and killing thousands of people. They warned that Utrecht, The Hague, and Amsterdam would follow. The Netherlands capitulated on 15 May, except Zeeland, in the southwest, where fighting continued; the Germans destroyed one of the most beautiful buildings of the country, Middelburg's town hall, in an air raid on 17 May, when the rest of the country was already under their rule. The Queen and the government had escaped in time to England, a wise move, although the first reaction of many Dutch people was a feeling of abandonment.

Bep went immediately to Rotterdam after the surrender with clothes, blankets, and food for her sister and brother-in-law and their nine children. They were all unharmed and even their house was undamaged. She returned home and life followed its normal course again. Schools and universities reopened their doors, cinemas, theatres, and concert halls finished the season more or less as planned, and apart from the destruction caused by the short war, and the presence of German soldiers, not much seemed to have changed.

In June, Corrie wrote her admission exam for the gymnasium and was accepted. It was a vindication of Flip's confidence in her, and a festive occasion, the prelude to a wonderful year. She knew the school from the stories her sisters had told over the years, but being there herself was a quite different experience. The teachers seemed to know her because of her sisters. The teacher of German called her *Die dritte Ausgabe* (the third edition), and everybody loved it when she played *quatre-mains* with a very tall blonde girl at a school concert. One teacher said to Tineke, "Your little sister is so cute, one would love to take her on one's lap." When Tineke reported this at home, Corrie was not pleased.

Flip and Bep tried to protect their daughters as much as they could, and for Corrie, at least, their efforts paid off. It was, of course, impossible to hide completely what was going on: the dismissal of Jewish teachers and professors in the fall; the student protest at Leiden University after which the university was closed by the German authorities; the dockworkers' strike in Amsterdam against the German anti-Jewish measures. But Corrie was so involved in her new school that she did not pay much attention to the outside world. When, one day, a boy from a

Dutch Nazi family who lived in the neighbourhood jeered at her, calling her a "filthy rotten Jew," it was a brutal blow that upset her and that she tried to forget.

When Flip was no longer allowed to have a car and was ordered to sell his at a low price, he softened the blow by proposing to buy a sailboat with the money he received from the sale. When the whole family went to a wharf at Zaandam, a few kilometres northwest of Amsterdam, to choose a boat, it was a festive outing, although I wonder what Flip and Bep were thinking. A friend with whom Flip used to play tennis had offered to register the boat in his name, as measures against the Jews were becoming ever more restrictive. Tineke, who was a member of the sea scouts, taught the rest of the family how to sail, and after their sailing trips they ate tiny apricot tarts decorated with real cream at a bakery shop in Aalsmeer, proud of their discovery at a time when such non-rationed luxuries had virtually disappeared. The days on the water were happy interludes in a summer during which the Germans and the Dutch Nazis brutally showed their true colours.

Bep's health did not improve: she was diagnosed as having thyroid problems. The family doctor prescribed rest and good food. It was like telling someone in the desert that a good swim and drinking lots of liquids would help to fight dehydration. Even without her disease, Bep would have been tense and nervous because of the increasing harassment and threats the Jews were subjected to by the Germans and their Dutch accomplices, of whom a great number had been given key positions in the police forces, the justice system, and the civil administration. While the first measures, though ominous, had seemed fairly harmless and not too difficult to cope with, slowly but surely the German grip grew tighter to the point of being unbearable. Even the summer outings to the lake near Aalsmeer were risky and had probably become ventures into forbidden territory. The registration of all Jews had been carried out with the help of meticulous civil servants who were not used to disobeying orders, no matter whence they came. Then, when all Dutch men and women fifteen years and older were given identity cards that they had to carry with them at all times, the Jews received theirs marked with a J. This happened in the latter half of 1941, when only Corrie was still under age. In retrospect, we wonder what would have happened if Bep, whose papers had been destroyed when the city hall of Middelburg burned down, had not let herself be registered as Jewish. Corrie sometimes dreams about the different life she would have had, but I think that it would not have made a difference, for in the Netherlands people know too much about each other's background for such a change of identity to succeed. Anyway, it is useless to speculate, for Bep was dutifully registered like the rest of the family. In June, the Germans declared beaches, swimming pools, and parks out of bounds for Jews, who were also barred from renting rooms in hotels and guest houses in tourist resorts and from horse races. Sailing was probably illegal, too, but as it was not explicitly mentioned, they took the risk of engaging in it.

By the end of August, it became impossible to keep up the appearance of a normal life. Jewish students were no longer admitted to schools where non-Jews also went. Corrie, who had so much liked the Haarlem Gymnasium, was forced to go to a hastily created Jewish high school where, because few students came from classical high schools, Greek and Latin were not taught. She was unhappy in her new school and felt lonely and disoriented. For Tineke, who was in the highest grade, a special arrangement was made so that she and two boys who were in the same situation could prepare for the examinations at the end of the new school year 1941-42. Towards the end of the winter, when Jews were no longer tolerated in the coastal zone and ordered to move to Amsterdam, Tineke received a temporary permit to stay in Haarlem at the house of the friend who had also helped out by registering the sailboat in his name. After receiving her high school diploma, thanks to the benevolent authorities, she rejoined the family, who by then had grown accustomed to their new living conditions.

The moving had been painful and emotionally draining. First the police had come to make an inventory of the contents of the house. Severe punishment would follow if any object was removed. Yet with the help of a family who owned a storage firm in Amsterdam but lived not far from Bep and Flip, their fine antique pieces of furniture were stacked away in a warehouse and replaced by cheap ones. These friends were genuinely altruistic, unlike many so-called helpers who did not want to return anything to the few owners who survived the

Occupation. A sideboard and a miniature desk in our house in Toronto are a reminder of this small triumph in what was a losing battle against the Germans.

Inexorably, the date of departure came nearer, and on a wet cold day Flip, Bep, Tineke, and Corrie walked with whatever belongings could be packed in a few suitcases to the nearby stop of the electric tramway from Zandvoort to Amsterdam, where they would board a special car. The organization was flawless. Police sealed the house the moment the family walked out the front door, the tram was on time, and their arrival in Amsterdam was in accordance with whatever plan may have existed for resettling the Jews living in the coastal region. It was in a sense a blessing that Flip's mother had died the year before, and so did not witness the decline and destruction of everything her son had built. For many months the house stood empty. Corrie even sneaked in once through a cellar trap door, together with a non-Jewish friend with whom she was staying one weekend. It was an eerie experience to be in the familiar surroundings and yet to feel like an intruder. She took a wastebasket she had always liked, gathered a few other beloved objects, and then the two girls left the house the same way they had entered. Nobody had noticed them, and the dangerous escapade did not have any untoward consequences. Back in Amsterdam, Corrie told her parents about her visit. They were not angry, but said she must promise not to go there again.

Even without such a promise, she could not have repeated her "break-in." Visiting her friend in Haarlem became impossible soon afterwards, when Jews were ordered to wear the yellow star and were barred from using any form of public transport. In the summer, the house was taken over by the *Organisation Todt* (which was responsible for military engineering), and was used as its regional headquarters. A large dark circle in the hardwood floor downstairs in the hall still shows where stood the beer barrel for the thirsty Germans.

Everything is relative, and among the victims of the resettlement Flip and his family belonged to those who considered themselves fortunate, having an address to go to where they were welcomed with open arms. Uncle Piet Wiener, a first cousin of Bep's, with whom she had grown up like brother and sister in Middelburg, lived in a spacious apartment in a quiet neighbourhood of Amsterdam with his wife, Aunt Zus, their son who was Corrie's age, and two younger daughters, Ied and Annemarie. Their son, Jan Dik, had been my classmate and friend for eight years, before the Jewish students were segregated. They had moved to that apartment shortly before, and I visited him there only once. I remember feeling awkward and helpless, confronted with the desperation that was obvious in spite of the family's effort not to show it. I never returned, thus missing the opportunity to meet Corrie's parents. I do not think they were already there when I came, as my visit most likely took place in the fall of 1941.

Even if I had been more faithful to my friend, I might not have met Bep and Flip, for they had been given the first floor as a separate apartment, while their hosts kept the upstairs rooms for themselves. The kitchen in the basement was shared, and on many occasions the two families had meals together. There was no garden but, when travelling became impossible, Piet and Zus rented an allotment in a garden complex on the outskirts of the city. For Corrie, who loved the outdoors, that garden became a cherished refuge from the brick and concrete of Amsterdam. But not for long. One day, when Corrie had gone to the garden ahead of the others, she discovered a sign at the main entrance to the garden that read "Jews not allowed." She panicked. Racing back home, she fell on the gravel path and hurt her knee. Bep cleaned the wound, dressed it, and tried to comfort her. Corrie eventually calmed down, the garden remained out of bounds, and that was the end of that.

So the Frenkels were literally trapped in Amsterdam, and for Corrie life revolved more than ever around school and home. Unlike the Jewish school in Haarlem, which in spite of good teachers had a makeshift character, the newly created Jewish high school in Amsterdam had an impressive teaching staff and a complete program, including Latin and Greek. It was located in a building formerly occupied by an elementary school, opposite the Orthodox Jewish High School that existed long before the war. In the first year of operation, the Jewish Lyceum, as it was called, offered many of its students some relief from the tense atmosphere at home. The teachers were remarkable in their efforts to stress the importance of learning and at the same time to create as pleasant a classroom atmosphere as possible. Corrie particularly enjoyed the history lessons of Mr. Presser. Although she had never liked history before, and would never like it again, thanks to the Jewish Lyceum she knows that history, well-taught, can be fascinating. Mr. Presser, who survived the war and later taught modern history at the University of Amsterdam, wrote extensively about the destruction of Dutch Jewry. The school has a place in his writings. He describes the clash between, on the one hand, the traditional role of the teacher who stresses the need to do the homework, to pay attention in class, and to be well prepared for tests, and on the other, the overwhelming sense of the futility of it all in light of the German agenda.

The level of fearful apprehension rose considerably when the yellow star was introduced, but it was not until the Germans sent out the first orders to show up for work in Germany or the occupied territories in the East that people started to panic. After the summer break—vacation being too positive a term—school resumed, but many students did not return. Among them was Anne Frank, who had been in the same grade as Corrie's cousin Ied. She belonged to those who went into hiding. Another group met their destiny in the extermination camps, about the existence of which vague rumours had started to circulate. Some families, when faced with deportation, committed suicide. The number of students gradually dwindled. Almost every day there were additional empty seats in the classrooms. Together with the demoralizing effect this had on the remaining children, there were the physical hardships of simply going to school. Because Jews were forbidden to use public transport and were not allowed to have bicycles, the only way to get to class was on foot. For those like Corrie, who lived far away, this meant an expedition of about an hour twice a day, with the risk of running into a street raid when the Germans arrested whoever happened to be wearing a yellow star.

It was not easy to carry all the books for a day, together with a lunch consisting of bread and jars of potato salad or beans, fruit being strictly forbidden to Jews. A classmate of Corrie's, Tijn de Jong, a remarkably cheerful boy, teamed up with her to devise what they thought to be a wonderful solution. They packed their books and lunches in an old doll carriage, and attached a long rope to it so that they could pull it along, taking turns. On smooth asphalt their method of transport was excellent, but they ran into trouble when the street surface was uneven. One day, they thought of getting around that problem by walking on the streetcar tracks between the rails. At a given moment, the carriage tipped to one side and the inevitable happened: it fell over, spreading its contents on the tracks. With fits of laughter Tijn and Corrie were collecting their things when a streetcar arrived. It had to wait a few minutes until the two children wearing yellow stars were finished. The whole scene looked like one of defiance, but there were no hostile reactions and they were allowed to continue on their way to school. Corrie remembers the doll carriage fondly, as if it were an innocent school prank.

The same cannot be said of another event that happened at about the same time. On the way to her math teacher's house for some extra help, Corrie saw her history teacher walking on the sidewalk, looking very tense and nervous, wringing his hands. He did not see her. She turned her head in the direction of his intent stare and saw a group of Jews, including his wife, who had been rounded up in the street and were being taken away by German police. He seemed to hesitate between joining her or running away. Corrie did not wait to see him decide. She walked on as fast as she could without running, more or less covering her yellow star with her schoolbag.

Such experiences became more and more common, and for many families the moment had come to make a crucial choice: go into hiding, comply with the order to show up for work in the East, let oneself be caught in a raid—resulting similarly in deportation—or try to obtain a special permit to stay in Amsterdam or elsewhere in the Netherlands. The Germans played a clever game of cat and mouse with their victims by creating a confusing array of temporary exemptions from resettlement, continuously declaring invalid lists of names of protected people and creating new short-lived loopholes. The Jewish Council, created by the Germans to administer Jewish affairs, was soon to play a key role in the deportations by doing most of the administrative work and helping the Germans considerably by drawing up the lists of those who were to be sent east. As a reward for their work, members of the Council were exempted *bis auf weiteres* (until further notice). It did not take long before the Council was despised and mistrusted by almost everybody, even those who tried to get its help in prolonging their stay in Amsterdam.

From the few scant remarks heard after the war, it appears that Flip was involved in the Council for a very short period. He must have withdrawn from it almost immediately. I assume that he thoroughly mistrusted anything the Germans promised and realized how they used and exploited the Council. This mistrust also kept him and Bep from applying for special status and going to what became known as "Barneveld" or "the Schaffelaar." A high-ranking Dutch bureaucrat, Mr. Frederiks, who collaborated with the Germans, "in order to prevent something worse from happening," was one of the very few who did indeed make an effort to help some Jews. He managed to obtain permission for some people, of the elite, to be interned in an estate, the Schaffelaar, near the village of Barneveld in the centre of the country. The lucky ones who were accepted there received the assurance that they would never have to leave the Netherlands, and they were even allowed to take some furniture and books to their place of internment. Uncle Piet and his family were to leave for Barneveld at the end of December 1942. It may have helped them that he and Mr. Frederiks had grown up in Zeeland and knew each other. Bep, too, could have played the Zeeland card, but she and Flip thought it was improbable that such a concentration of Jews in one place—the Barneveld population grew eventually to more than six hundred—would be left alone by the Germans. They were right, and yet....

The question for Corrie, Tineke, and their parents—Tilie, the oldest daughter, was not in Amsterdam; an independent young woman of twenty-one makes her own decisions—was not whether, but when, to go into hiding. On 19 December the die was cast, and they were left no choice. Every day Flip still went to his office. What kind of work a Jewish lawyer could do in those days without running into trouble with the authorities is hard for me to imagine. Whatever he was busy with, he was in his office on the afternoon of 19 December 1942 when two members of the *Grüne Polizei* (Green Police—called this because of the colour of their uniforms) came to arrest him. They knew a lot about him; his pre-war assistance to many refugees was no secret to them. Corrie thinks that they even knew that he was prepared to go into hiding, but it seems more likely to me that they were bluffing, assuming that this was his most probable choice. Flip knew the scenario that would follow. After having taken him to a temporary prison, they would go and collect the other members of the family in order to send them all to the transit camp and then to Poland. So Flip started the most important plea he ever made. He pointed out that Jews were not criminals and that the Germans were wrong in treating them as such. Fluent in German, he spoke for a long time, maybe an hour, and was so convincing that the two young Germans, in spite of themselves, listened attentively. When Flip had finished, they said that they would return the next morning and left.

Meanwhile, after a long wait filled with anxiety, for when somebody was late one involuntarily thought of all the horrible things that could have happened, the family had started dinner. The main course—exceptional for those days—was mussels. They had barely begun the meal when Flip arrived, shaken and pale. He was able, though, to report coherently what had happened, concluding by saying that the Germans had obviously given them a chance to go into hiding. A short consultation with Uncle Piet and Aunt Zus followed. Should they wait until the next morning? Would it not be too dangerous for those who were still in the house when the Germans did not find Bep, Flip, and their daughters there? Uncle Piet said he and Aunt Zus were willing to take that risk, and that he thought it safer for them to leave immediately. So they took their leave, and went hastily to an emergency address. The mussels, the last meal they ate together as a family, were never finished.

Lilies of the Valley and Asparagus
1942-45

IN THE DAYS LEADING to our wedding, Corrie and I had to decide whom to choose as witnesses, and although we had an *embarras du choix*, we easily agreed who would sign our papers with us. First, there was Tilie, who together with Herbert had taken over the role of Corrie's parents after the war, and Bertus, my sister's husband, who had given me his hospitality and friendship in the confusing student years that are supposed to be carefree, but that for me had been anything but. We also asked Uncle Nico Bink, who had sheltered Corrie during the war and had warmly invited her to stay with his family until she finished high school in 1947. Finally there was Rob van Schaik, my best friend from high school. With great solicitude he had helped me come out of a deep depression at the end of my university studies. Even the choice of a notary was no problem. I wanted to go to the somewhat eccentric father of a classmate, but Tilie and Herbert pointed out that a good friend of Corrie's father would certainly feel hurt if we passed him by. We agreed, and so one day we went to his office in a beautiful old house on one of the canals. He made some rather clichéd remarks about generations and friendship and charged us the normal fee. I did not like him, even though Corrie had spent the first night of her underground existence under his roof.

Corrie does not have fond memories of that first night in hiding, sleeping together with Tineke in a narrow bed, but at least they were more or less safe there. Early the next morning, the two sisters went their separate ways. Corrie went all by herself to the Central Station, for the first time in months without the yellow star. She took the train to Baarn, a small town not far from Utrecht, situated in one of the few wooded areas in the west of the country. Former neighbours had moved to the Baarn area when the father became the director of a dairy there. When they opened the door at half past seven in the morning and saw Corrie, they were not happy. A promise of help lightly made, with the thought that things would never become so bad that help would indeed be needed, was now obviously regretted. Yet Corrie was taken in, and she shared in the Christmas celebrations with a red gelatin and real fruit pudding and lots of whipped cream. Her fifteenth birthday, a few days later, went by unnoticed. One could not blame her hosts for the oversight, because Corrie herself had kept silent about what, for Dutch people, is such an important day. There were three boys in the family, all older than Corrie and well-disposed to her, and one daughter, younger than she and not easy to get along with, being rather spoilt. The mother—in fact the stepmother—was the children's governess, apparently preferred by the father to his first wife.

Corrie felt lost and unhappy. She probably would have felt that way anywhere, brutally torn away as she was from her family. In Baarn there was no real warmth, and, rightly or wrongly, she had the impression that her hosts would be glad to see her leave. Perhaps the "address," as refuges were called in the Resistance, was meant to be temporary all along—Corrie is not sure—but in any event, she did not stay long in Baarn, and was moved to a much smaller village south of Apeldoorn.

It was an abrupt transition from the affluence of a factory director's household to near poverty in Eerbeek, where a former domestic of the Frenkel family, who had looked after the children before Corrie was born, had a small grocery store. Her husband's barbershop was in the same house, and they had five children, the oldest of whom was a boy of nine. The Frenkel family had been fond of Tuitje, as they called her, but Corrie did not know her or the other family members. Living under one roof with them was not easy. For the parents, who were very busy during the day, it was a welcome change to have somebody to look after the children. Their nine year old was quite a handful, unruly and disobedient, and Corrie was often exhausted by the end of the day. She liked it best when she could take the children out into the woods or wander through the fields with them. One day, when she was far away from home, a fierce thunderstorm drenched them. In a panic she rushed home with her flock, carrying the youngest child, only to be sternly scolded upon arrival by the father, who was extremely worried. He called her irresponsible and stupid for not having noticed the threatening clouds.

In normal circumstances such a scolding would be unpleasant enough; in a situation of total dependence on the goodwill of the people who sheltered her at serious risk to themselves, it was devastating. It reinforced Corrie's insecurity and loneliness, a combination of the awkwardness most people experience in their teens exacerbated by a sense of being in danger and of threatening the safety of the people with whom she was staying. She managed to suppress these feelings most of the time, but deep down they were always there.

The danger of being discovered was far from imaginary in the small village; people started to wonder where the dark girl who was supposed to be a temporary helper came from, and how long she would stay. Marietje, Tilie's friend who throughout the war helped the Frenkel family as much as she could, and Corrie's parents, with whom Marietje was in touch regularly, worried a good deal about Corrie's safety, and tried to find a better solution. Corrie was unaware of what was going on behind the scenes and lived in limbo. Afterwards it was very hard for her to remember the chronology of events, and there are strange gaps in her recollections. She is almost sure that she once visited her parents in the summer of 1943, but it is also possible that she heard so much about their hideout in a tent, and wished so much to be there with them, that wish and reality fused. Neither can she remember a visit by a former classmate that must have taken place in 1943 or 1944. The two friends lost sight of each other, and it was only in the late 1980s that Gerda van Leeuwen, who now lives in New Orleans, asked during a school reunion of the Haarlem Gymnasium about her friend. She phoned Corrie immediately and they now write regularly, and have met several times. Gerda has a picture she took of Corrie during the 1940s and Corrie even recognized the clothes she was wearing in it. Neither of them can recall what happened and where, but Gerda remembers vividly having lost a beautiful little purse her mother had lent her for the trip to see Corrie. Why Gerda was given the secret address, while secrecy was crucial, and by whom, remains a mystery. Trying to reconstruct the past, they are both convinced that it could only have been in Rotterdam that they saw each other.

Thanks to Ada Varekamp, the history teacher at the Montessori High School in Rotterdam, a new address was found for Corrie. Ada, an orphan, had been the protegée of Uncle Piet's sister Mies, who taught history at a high school for girls in The Hague. Corrie's parents must have suggested that someone ask Ada for help, hoping that she was involved in underground work, or would at least know whom to approach. Ada had no ideas, but reviewed in her mind the students she had taught over the years, or was teaching at the moment, and took a gamble. She asked the parents of two students, a sister and brother, whether they were willing to take in a girl about the same age as their son. They said they would have been happy to accept her, but a few days before Ada's visit they had promised an organization that helped Jews to open their house to an old lady. They were expecting her any day. A week later they let Ada know that the arrangement with the old lady had fallen through, and that Corrie was most welcome. Did this mean that another address had been found or, more likely, that the Germans had caught yet another victim, whose death meant Corrie's salvation?

Meeting total strangers is never without tension. For the third time, the fifteen-year-old girl who had been put outside the law would have to depend entirely on the good will and courage of people she did not know. The first encounter with them was stressful. She feared the moment the front door would open, although her fear was mixed with resignation. One of the first things Corrie was told by her hostess—who soon became Aunt Bap to Corrie—was that she had always wanted more children. Her husband, Uncle Nico, told Corrie that he had studied law in Utrecht like her father, whom he had not known, but whose thesis he had read and admired. Both were compassionate and friendly, never even hinting that they were taking great risks in hiding her. They were united in their abhorrence of the racial policies of the Germans, whom they loathed. For the rest, one could not imagine two people more different from each other. He was a tall, impressive man with a stern face, a deep voice, strong-willed and dominant. His short, typically Dutch surname, Bink, perfectly suited his personality. She was tiny, frail, and hunchbacked, a deformity that made breathing difficult.

She was soft-spoken and shy, and often tried to hush up the heated debates that tended to degenerate into unpleasant quarrels. She came from an impoverished noble family, descendants of Swiss-Huguenot gentry. Berthe Elise Louise de Senarclens de Grancy had met Nicolaas Johannes Bink while they were both studying law at Utrecht. He had joined a law firm in Rotterdam, where they bought a house in a quiet residential district. During vacations, they went with their two children to the family estate in the south of the country, where Aunt Bap had grown up.

Shortly after coming to Rotterdam—it must have been at Whitsun, 1943—Corrie accompanied them to the old country estate for the first time. The main house, built in 1649, was like a small French castle, with a bridge over a small river, a gate, and a courtyard, in the middle of which stood the tallest tree with the biggest trunk she had ever seen. There was a coach house on one side of the courtyard; on the other side was a large garden. A broad lane led from the house to the end of the formal garden, where the kitchen garden began. On both sides of the lane old beech trees formed a shaded tunnel, referred to as the *berceau*. A few thatched-roof farmhouses also belonged to the property. A winding stream, the Dommel, flowed to the Maas, and under beautiful trees an abundance of lilies of the valley was blooming. Corrie, who had never been in that part of the country, almost lost all sense of reality. The trip from Rotterdam by boat and the last stretch in a horse-drawn carriage—one of the farmers of the estate had come to meet them at the landing stage of the carrier service—was like a fairy tale. Later Corrie returned there many times. She loved working in the garden and the kitchen garden. She also helped the farmers with the rye harvest and worked in the asparagus beds. The shoots of the white asparagus were to be cut with a special triangular knife, as soon as a crack in the soil indicated that an asparagus was ready to be harvested, before it saw daylight and turned purple.

The pastoral, idyllic life with an old-fashioned, nineteenth-century flavour seemed light-years away from the outside world of food shortages, persecutions, and deportations. Even though the Germans had set up a prison for hostages (mostly political dissidents) at St. Michielsgestel, a kilometre east of the estate, and a concentration camp for both

Jews and non-Jews at Vught nearby to the west, Corrie felt protected and freer than she had been in a long time. Back in Rotterdam, however, more precautions were necessary, and she stayed mostly inside, spending many hours with Aunt Bap, knitting or sewing, quietly sitting in the sunroom overlooking the garden. They grew very fond of each other, a fact that was soon noticed by the daughter, three years older than Corrie, who was in a rebellious phase in her relationship with her parents. She became jealous of the new girl, and sometimes had outbursts of hostility to which Corrie reacted by withdrawing into herself. Corrie loved playing the piano, but after once hearing the older girl say, "This is my piano," she no longer attempted to play. Happily, in adulthood, nothing was left of the friction that characterized that initial period of their acquaintanceship.

It is doubtful that Corrie would have asked for piano lessons, because she had trouble asking for anything for herself. She did not even mention the orthodontic treatment that was unfinished when she went into hiding. Her foster parents, Uncle Nico and Aunt Bap, began to worry about her health because she was so quiet and ate so little. They thought she might have tuberculosis, and arranged for her to be examined by their family doctor. He did not find anything, and said that the problem was psychological. Uncle Nico was convinced that Corrie needed a more normal life. He reasoned that being cooped up in the house for long, empty days, worrying about her sisters and her parents, was having an adverse effect on her mental and physical health. Having thought it over, and undoubtedly after discussing it with his wife, he came up with an ingenious plan that was to have a dramatic impact on Corrie's life.

Uncle Nico was very bright, and a courageous man of action. At City Hall, he knew a man who worked in the civic registry department and whom he trusted. He went to see him and more or less dictated him fabricated data about Corrie's identity, telling him to ask no further questions. Thus, as Vili Cornelia Scherer, Corrie "became" the daughter of Vili Vidòr, originally from Hungary, and Herman Scherer, an actual distant relative of Aunt Bap's. In Uncle Nico's account, Herman Scherer was born in the town of Semarang, in the Dutch East Indies, on August 3, 1901. He married Vili Vidòr and they had a daughter, Vili Cornelia, on March 28, 1929. The family moved back to Holland when Vili Cornelia

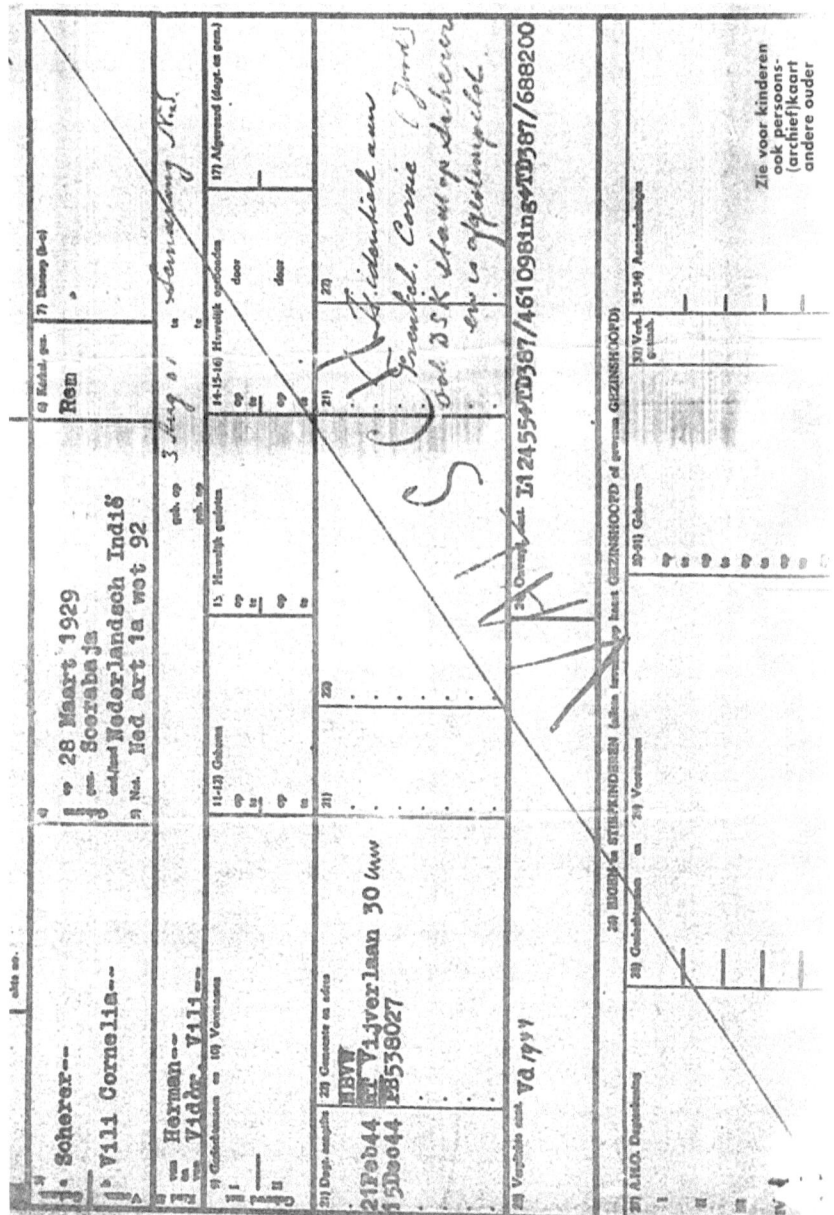

Corrie's registration under a new name.

The Curtain

Document returning Corrie to her old name.

was about three years old. The Scherers lived near Haarlem, but during an air raid their house was destroyed and somehow, by coincidence, the family papers at the Haarlem registry were lost as well. The Binks had taken the daughter into their home temporarily. Now almost fifteen, the girl would soon need an identity card. Thanks to this plan, Corrie kept her own first name and became fifteen months younger. Her dark complexion was now presumed to be the result of an exotic love affair of long-bygone times, not unusual in families who had lived in the tropics for several generations.

In 1996, a friend of ours made inquiries at the Rotterdam registry at our request. Officials there unearthed the documents concerning Vili Cornelia Scherer. After the war, steps were taken to help Corrie get back her own identity. The document stating the return to her pre-war name bears the correction as well as a diagonal line parallel to which the word *valsch* (false) has been handwritten; *valsch* follows the spelling that predates the Dutch spelling reforms of 1934, when the *ch* was abolished, and Dutch *vals* became less similar to German *falsch*. It is also stated on the document that "Scherer, Vili Cornelia, is 'identiek aan' (is identical to) Frenkel, Corrie Jood (Jew)." One wonders what kind of a civil servant wrote in such a way even after Liberation. It looks as if he was irritated that the almost flawless administration had been fooled by somebody with no sense of duty. After the war Corrie would have liked to thank the man with no sense of duty. She could not, though, because the Germans had executed him when they found out about his role in the Resistance.

Once Corrie had regained legal status, she could move freely in the city and anywhere else she wanted to go, but apart from doing some errands or helping with the shopping, which became more and more difficult as the war continued, there was not much for her to do. The next step towards a normal life was to register her in a high school. The Montessori High School was the obvious choice. The Binks had sent their own children there, and Ada Varekamp was not only the school's history teacher but also lived with the principal, Miss de Haan, who taught Dutch. A very important consideration was that none of the teachers at the school had pro-German inclinations and that the students almost exclusively came from upper-middle-class families with progressive ideas about education and a loathing of Nazi ideology. The principal was willing to accept Corrie, but there was a snag, and the whole plan almost fell through.

The Montessori High School, or the High School for Montessori Pupils, as Maria Montessori, the creator of the educational philosophy, had stipulated it be called, was not open to everyone. Students who did not meet the requirement of having been at a Montessori elementary school could apply, and their cases would then be discussed at a plenary session of the teachers together with the members of the school board. Ada and her friend were on edge when the collective mood of the meeting seemed to turn negative. But one of the members of the board came to the rescue. She could not resist the temptation to show that she was not fooled by what the meeting had been told about Corrie, and at the same time she wanted to cut the knot: "I think we should accept that 'black child' of the Binks." For Ada and Miss de Haan, there was a moment of anxiety, but nobody asked any further questions.

So, after an interruption of many months, Corrie went back to school. She never made a mistake about her new identity. Only once, when she and her friends were daydreaming about travelling after the war, and talking about cruises, she almost slipped: "Oh, I would love to go on a long voyage!" Her classmates reacted with surprise, "But you are the only one of us who has been on such a trip, when you came from the East Indies to Holland!" Corrie reacted immediately to repair any possible damage: "Yeah, but that doesn't count. I was too young to remember."

The first few weeks at the new school were bewildering. Used to an old-fashioned grammar school and eager to get on with learning and make up for lost time, Corrie was quite disappointed to arrive at the beginning of "Swedish week." Following the principles of the Montessori method, all lessons that week, as far as possible, concentrated on Sweden. The students were divided into groups and did research, and created objects from available materials for an exhibition of maps, flags, and Swedish art. Everybody was very friendly, though, and willing to help her settle in. The relationship between teachers and students was very different from what she had been used to. After the first months, Corrie became a Montessori convert and discovered that, even though the approach was very different from the one she was used to, the students did learn a lot. She came to love the informal and friendly atmosphere.

Thus life had become almost normal, but not quite. The absence of her family and the worries about their fate made her cling to the few objects she had brought with her. In later years she felt ashamed that she did not want anybody else to use her sheets from home. These two sheets had been packed by her mother along with her clothes.

Twice she saw members of her family. The first occasion was a happy one; the second was not. Bep, Corrie's mother, was a courageous woman who was willing to take risks to see her daughter. As a rule, the Resistance network was adamantly opposed to people in their care visiting each other and thus increasing the risk of detection. Yet, irresponsible or daring, such reunions did take place, and for Corrie, her mother's visit in Rotterdam is one of her most precious memories of those dark years. For Bep, it must have been an uplifting experience to see her youngest daughter in the good care of the Bink family. Corrie even remembers her mother overhearing her telephone conversation with a friend about ballroom dancing lessons that she and her schoolmates were engaged in. These Saturday night classes took place at different people's homes. In those moments, it seemed as if there was no war.

The second reunion was with Tineke, after the girls had been warned by a coded telegram that something had gone wrong for their parents. Seeing each other again was a small consolation in their distress. As arranged, both sisters went to Marietje's parents' house. From this emergency address, Corrie went for a short while to a young couple who had already taken in an older Jewish woman. They were expecting their first baby and were very friendly to Corrie, who was nevertheless relieved when the underground workers decided it was safe for her to return to Rotterdam.

Burdened with the extra worry about her father and mother, now that they had fallen into the hands of the Germans, she resumed the life of a teenager. With the help of a young couple who were classicists, and later confessed that they secretly called her "Corrie *submersa*," she caught up with her classmates in Latin and Greek. We will never know how many others guessed that she was, as the Dutch said in those days, an *onderduiker* (someone who has dived under). If anyone did, nobody ever asked her or the Binks about it, and, more importantly, nobody denounced her to the Germans. So Corrie made it, undisturbed, until the end of the war.

Undisturbed is not actually the right word. The last winter was full of upheaval and difficulties. These conditions, however, were the same for everybody, and had nothing to do with being Jewish. The summer of 1944 had been beautiful in the countryside—lush, sunny, and full of encouraging news about the Allied troops advancing through northern France and Belgium. As the Allies approached the Netherlands at the end of August, the Binks had to make a quick decision. Should the family stay on the country estate or return to Rotterdam? Because of Uncle Nico's work, and classes starting in September, Rotterdam won. They hurried back to the city, a few days before the Canadians reached the border between Belgium and the Netherlands, and hoped that it would soon be Rotterdam's turn to be liberated.

They had to wait nine long months before that day came. It was an endless, dark, and bitterly cold winter. Thanks to the farmers on the estate, the Binks, until then, always had some supplements to the official rations. Each time they returned from the country to Rotterdam, they brought back flour, potatoes, butter, bacon, and eggs, so that they had never felt the need to build up reserve supplies for emergencies. Now they were suddenly cut off from the estate, which was in the very middle of the battle front. The Bink family thus had a particularly hard time in the famine winter of 1944-45. Corrie's aversion to eating, which started in Baarn, had lingered on, but now her unconsciously determined revolt against her fate ceased to make sense. Everybody was equal in not having enough to eat and in being constantly hungry.

Even in the darkest hours there were some cheerful distractions. An ingenious invention literally brought a little light into the living room. A bicycle on a stand with a small dynamo on the front wheel and wires connected to a small light bulb above the table, and another above the handlebars, made it possible for people to read. Everybody except Aunt Bap took turns pedalling. The person pedalling had the advantage of having the handlebar light all to him- or herself. Especially at first, everybody found the sight of the pedaller and the two tiny lights hilarious, and of course it boosted morale. Later on in the winter and early spring of 1945, it became obvious even to the most inveterate pessimists that the war was almost over and that the Germans had lost. When Allied planes dropped food for the starving population of the big cities in the west of the country, Corrie was among the volunteers who sorted out the contents of the often smashed containers. She and the other volunteers worked in a factory and as a special treat were given a good lunch. Food was still so scarce, and the temptation to smuggle some of it out of the building so great, that everybody was frisked at the exit. One day, however, Corrie was allowed to take home a small bag with a mixture of tea leaves and powdered egg. This mixture was so difficult to separate that even the hospitals could not use it. For Aunt Bap, who had missed real tea very much and who was very patient, it was a wonderful gift.

A few days after Liberation, Herbert, Tilie's boyfriend, who had escaped to England and joined the army, came to see Corrie. As a soldier of the Allied forces, he had been able to travel to Rotterdam after having found out where his future youngest sister-in-law lived. He brought news from Tilie and Tineke, with whom Corrie was reunited as soon as travel conditions allowed. Corrie went to the Red Cross many times to see whether her parents' names were on the lists of those who were repatriated from the German camps. For her, the war was not over. The most difficult time still lay ahead.

The Curtain
1942-44

In Toronto many of our friends remain for us without the background information we were used to in the Netherlands. Newcomers like us, they have left parents, brothers and sisters, and friends in their countries of origins. So what we see is what we know, and we receive glimpses of their past only once in a while, when they talk about their years back home.

For us, this absence of what could be called the setting where people belong is unusual. In the Netherlands, when people are introduced to each other, it rarely takes more than five minutes to discover common friends or acquaintances. In general we prefer the vacuum surrounding our friends—and this is also true for those born in Canada—compared to the overload of information we were used to in Holland. Therefore, contrary to our tradition, we do not even try to fill in the gaps when we meet Dutch people.

However, filling in the gaps is precisely what I have been trying to do, piecing together what happened to Corrie's parents, and with what choices they were faced when they were barely a few years older than our children are now.

At first only Tilie was separated from the family. She remained in Utrecht with her friends, after Jewish students were no longer allowed to continue their university studies. Travel without a yellow star became more and more dangerous, so visits to Amsterdam were too risky. In December 1942 she felt that the moment had come to go into hiding. She went from one address to another in the east of the country, then found shelter in the house of a doctor who lived in the south, near the Belgian border. She did not want to put anybody at risk, though, and against the advice of her underground contacts, who thought it too dangerous—but all the same provided her with an address in Brussels—she crossed the border. She remained in the Belgian capital, where life for Jews, despite the continuous threat, was somewhat less perilous than in the Netherlands, with its flawless civil registry and diligent, compliant bureaucracy.

The only one of the three sisters who was blonde, Tilie had a great advantage, and blended in with the nuns in a hospital where she found work as a nurse's aid. Herbert's parents also fled to Brussels and were liberated there by the Allied forces in 1944. Herbert himself and his younger brother went even further. They were given French papers by the Resistance movement of that country, which permitted them to cross Paris and go to Oloron. High in the Pyrenees mountains, exhausted and discouraged in awful weather, the younger brother wanted to give up, but Herbert dragged him along and they managed to reach Spain. From there they went to England and enlisted in a special detachment of the Dutch army in which some family members served. This was very important in a period during which contact with relatives was mostly impossible.

For Corrie, Tineke, and their parents, the real Diaspora began with the hasty departure from Uncle Piet and Aunt Zus's house after the unfinished evening meal on 19 December 1942. Communication between the members of the family was either cut off completely, as in Tilie's case, or very rare and not without risk. After the war, when the three sisters were reunited, they told each other what had happened to them during the years of forced separation, but they did not like to dwell on their experiences. Even now, when it has become less difficult for them to talk about the past, there are many gaps, and only once in a while an episode, never mentioned before, comes to the surface unexpectedly in a conversation.

In a way, Tineke's years of hiding were rather uneventful. Most of the time until Liberation she lived in Zeist, a quiet residential village outside Utrecht, in the house of the first wife of the principal of the Barlaeus Gymnasium in Amsterdam. Tineke was hardly ever allowed to leave the house, but she had access to the garden, where she had a favourite hideout, behind a low brick wall where passersby could not see her. Her hostess was extremely cautious. She did not want to arouse the curiosity of people in whose lives the discovery of a mysterious newcomer would be an event for endless talk. Nor did she appreciate a visit by Bep, which left Tineke feeling awkward. In the beginning, it was almost like solitary confinement. Later, in 1944, her hostess became less strict and she established some contacts for Tineke with the University of Utrecht. She was able to prepare for her first year-end exam in medical studies. Professors of the faculty cooperated wholeheartedly in the clandestine enterprise, and saw to it that a valid examination took place.

Compared to many others, the three sisters had been lucky, yet in order to get on with their lives after Liberation, they seemed to lock away the war years, preferring not to revive a past with which it was very difficult, if not impossible, to come to grips. Piecing together the fragments that surfaced and making them into a coherent whole has been a challenge, and I have often felt inadequate for the self-imposed task, although I have, on occasion, been able to ask them for further information. In the case of Flip and Bep, first-hand recollections were impossible, so the story of what happened to them can only be sketchy and shrouded in uncertainty.

To begin with, I do not know how long Flip and Bep stayed in Amsterdam after their flight from a pseudo-legal but lawless and perilous existence. The Germans who came to arrest them probably expected not to find them; they did not take Uncle Piet and his family as replacements and left empty-handed. It is not likely that they immediately tried to hunt down the fugitives. Nevertheless, Flip and Bep thought Amsterdam too dangerous as a locale for a hiding place, because of Flip's position as a lawyer in one of the city's old and prestigious law firms.

In spite of an extensive network of friendships going back to Flip's student days, temporary—let alone permanent—shelter turned out to be extremely elusive. Eventually they ended up in a rural area between the major rivers, as the Maas, the Waal, and the Rhine are called in Holland, in the house of a friend, Dr. van der Willigen, who, like many medical doctors in those days, not only had his practice at home but was also in charge of the pharmacy that served the region. There was a constant coming and going of people who needed the doctor's help, or who wanted a prescription. Even in his big house, there were no foolproof hiding places where a person could stay comfortably for long periods of time without being seen by curious patients and visitors. Maybe it would have been wise to accept that risk, but when a most unusual opportunity to move presented itself, Flip and Bep decided not to endanger their host and his family any longer, and put their fate in the hands of Teun, who was the absolute master over an area of marshland of dense alder and willow bushes and reed-lined, narrow ditches. Teun allowed them into his secret domain.

Secret it was indeed, almost impenetrable and inaccessible, except by rowboat. At the few places where the winding waterways seemed to invite adventurous rowers to explore the wetlands, stern No Trespassing signs warned against the consequences of such an endeavour. On a dry island under a canopy of alder, willow, and elderberry green, which was used as a duck decoy, Teun put up a tent for his new protegés. Walking along narrow trails, he brought them their meals, and sometimes he stayed for a while and chatted with them, telling them the latest news about the war. Apart from Teun's regular visits, the Frenkels received few guests (Corrie, Tineke, and Marietje did have occasion to visit), and nobody threatened their silent existence in what nature lovers would call a summer paradise. However, uncertainty about their daughters' fate, discouragement because of the seemingly endless war, and fear of being detected, combined with forced inactivity and a feeling of helplessness, changed this paradise into an oppressive prison. The Dutch term for duck decoy is *eendenkooi* (literally, "ducks' cage"), and decoy is itself a word borrowed from the Dutch *de kooi* (the cage). Bep and Flip were, indeed, in a cage from which it was impossible to escape; for them, even beyond the precincts of the decoy, prison-like conditions prevailed.

In order to occupy themselves during those long, lonely days, Bep smocked a piece of silk, part of an old curtain that she had taken with her, while Flip whittled small sculptures out of willow. In the primitive conditions of camping in the marshlands, life was reduced to the bare minimum for survival, but the decoy was a safe, almost ideal hiding place, because even the Germans respected the No Trespassing signs.

However, when the autumn leaves began to fall and the tent could no longer protect them against the damp, cold weather, it became obvious that changes had to be made. Teun, who had turned out to be very helpful and well-disposed, offered to buy wood and construct a small cabin. Even without the protection of dense foliage, it might be possible to find a location where the cabin could not be spotted from outside the decoy. The plan was rejected all the same, because of the heating problem. No matter how hidden the little construction would be, smoke would rise up into the sky and undoubtedly be noticed. Without a stove, Bep and Flip would fall ill and waste away.

Dr. van der Willigen was instrumental in finding a new address in a nearby village. Here Flip and Bep were dry and warm, but there were major disadvantages. It was too dangerous to venture outside, so the Frenkels were confined to the house, and even there they did not move freely, but stayed exclusively in the room that was normally only used on solemn occasions, such as a wedding or a funeral. For the family, most activities were concentrated in the kitchen. At the celebration of Herbert's seventy-fifth birthday in 1995, Marietje told me that she had visited Flip and Bep some time after they moved from Teun's domain. She had found them resigned and subdued but in fairly good spirits, although the forced inactivity weighed heavily upon them. It was clear that they accepted their new circumstances.

Unfortunately, the major danger now came from a factor over which they had no control. Their host was a typical wheeler-dealer, who had taken them in for the money rather than out of the conviction that Jews had to be protected from the Germans. Hosts for profit were less reliable than genuine Resistance workers, but as long as money was available there was no great risk of being thrown out or even denounced to the German authorities. Sheltering Jews was not the only source of fast profit, though. Their host was also active in the black market, especially in clandestine slaughtering and selling of meat.

One day in January 1944, six members of the Dutch State Police surrounded the house and started a search. They not only found what they were looking for but also came across two people who were unaccounted for in the registry. They grasped the situation immediately, and their reaction was unfortunately in line with what happened in a great number of similar cases. Five out of the six men were, as they stated afterwards, against the Germans and in favour of letting the two Jews escape. Yet they kept them captive for fear of being denounced by the sixth member of the search squad, who had National Socialist leanings. It is now useless to speculate about what would have happened if the overwhelming majority of so-called "good" Dutch people had taken a firm, principled stand against the Germans and their Dutch accomplices, and yet one wonders....

Dr. van der Willigen, informed about what had happened, alerted Corrie and Tineke, sending them—or rather, their hosts—an identical telegram: "The helmsman and his wife have gone on a trip." Following the instructions that had been agreed upon, the girls both went to Marietje, who found temporary addresses for them, as there was a real danger that the Germans, having caught the parents, would find out about the daughters and go after them. However, nothing happened, and after a few weeks they both went back to what they considered their permanent homes. Apparently, their parents had been prudent enough not to have any document, snippet of paper, or object that could lead the Germans to the girls. They did have a picture of their daughters, though. In 1938, during a family visit to Bep's native Zeeland, a series of photographs had been taken of the three girls in national dress. On the page in the album where those pictures were placed, there is still an empty spot. For how long Bep and Flip were able to keep the picture, I do not know. In their relentless efforts to dehumanize the existence of their victims, the Germans often confiscated photographs, the possession of which they declared a crime.

The Dutch police took their prisoners to the nearest detention prison in Arnhem. For Flip, as he wrote in a message on toilet paper smuggled out of the prison, the contact with his fellow prisoners, many of whom were intellectuals and all of whom were against the Germans, was a relief after the long months of isolation. He was, of course, worried about Bep, from whom he was separated, but he thoroughly enjoyed the conversations with the other inmates and the lectures they organized for each other.

They did not stay very long—about three weeks—in Arnhem, after which they were taken to Westerbork, the transit camp through which tens of thousands of Jews passed on their way to Poland. From Westerbork each Tuesday a cattle train with about a thousand Jews—men, women, and children, old people, young people, the sick, and the healthy—left for an unknown but dreaded destination. The inhabitants of the camp were kept "in storage," as the title of the diary of an inmate published after the war aptly states, before being shipped out according to schedules worked out by the German authorities in Berlin and in The Hague. Nobody knew precisely what happened in Poland, but there were enough portentous signs for everybody to want to stay in Westerbork as long as possible and not be put on the list for the next train. That such a situation did not bring out the best in people under constant threat of being deported goes without saying. Without influential friends or the possibility of giving presents surreptitiously to those in charge, the chances of a prolonged stay in the camp were slim. One category, though, was even worse off than those without any means: the ones who were caught while in hiding.

They were given an "S" on their papers (for *straf* [punishment]) and put in the S-barracks, always the one that provided an easy contingent for the transports. The inhabitants of the S-barracks were denied the privileges enjoyed by the other inmates, could not go to the concerts and shows that were organized, were not allowed outside the narrow precincts of their quarters, and thus found themselves in a prison inside a prison. The fact that Flip and Bep did not end up in the S-barracks and were not immediately deported to Poland has never been discussed in the family. Did they get rid of their punishment-stigma with the help of camp VIPs? Did Flip once more convince the Germans that he was not a criminal, or did they bribe the right person to keep them out of the penal hut? In retrospect it does not matter and it did not make much difference.

Westerbork was a strange place, full of contradictions. On the one hand, there was the German regime, harsh even without the extreme cruelty of other camps; there was also the greed, egoism, and cynicism of the prisoners, and the continuous threat of being separated from one's relatives and friends, of being torn away from one's country. On the other hand, Westerbork was the scene of unexpected reunions, of excellent medical care in the camp hospital, where there was sometimes almost a surplus of highly qualified specialists, and a place of altruism and self-sacrifice.

When Flip and Bep arrived in the camp, Uncle Piet, Aunt Zus, and their three children were there, as well as Bep's older sister Cor and her husband, Flip's older brother Lion, and seven of their nine children, the two oldest sons having gone into hiding. Flip had been right about the elite camp at Barneveld, where Piet and Zus and their children had gone, about ten days after the events of 19 December 1942. In spite of all the assurances about special status and protection, all the Barneveld people had been moved to Westerbork in the last days of September 1943, arriving at the same time as the remnants of the Jewish Council of Amsterdam and some other VIPs from the Jewish community who had, up till then, been exempted from deportation *bis auf weiteres*. Jan Dik, the son of Piet and Zus and my former classmate, wrote me a letter from Westerbork about schoolwork and the Latin and Greek texts he was reading. Hidden in the censored text was the remark that the former vice-principal of our gymnasium, Dr. de Vries, had left for the same place where Alex had gone a year and a half before.

Not all trains went directly to Auschwitz and Sobibor (a less-known but lethally efficient extermination camp); a few carried their load to Bergen-Belsen, where conditions were, according to the rumour mill, better than in Poland, or to Theresienstadt (Terezín), in Czechoslovakia, which was supposed to be almost like a spa. Everything in the world of the camps was relative, and Theresienstadt, although the ultimate in camp luxury, was overcrowded and filthy. Yet it had an active cultural life with concerts, plays, and operas—and even performances of new compositions written there—and families with young children were allowed to stay together. No matter how different Theresienstadt was, though, it shared one aspect of the inmates' lives with Westerbork and many other camps: sealed cattle trains, full of people, left there regularly for Auschwitz, and the Germans played the same cat-and-mouse game with their victims as everywhere else. Even so, people who were in Theresienstadt considered themselves lucky, and hoped to bide their time till the end of the war. Bep and Flip arrived in Theresienstadt before Piet and Zus were sent there. Aunt Zus told us, on at least two occasions, how Corrie's mother had welcomed the exhausted and dishevelled family, and because they had not yet been given a place to stay, had given her own bed to her so that she could sleep and recover somewhat from the transport. Lion and Cor and their seven children had also ended up in the camp, so the family, except for those in hiding, was united again.

One would expect that with so many people around, it would be easy to form an idea of how Flip and Bep fared during the second-last stop of their journey. However, those who came back did not talk very much about their camp existence, and hardly ever mentioned Corrie's parents. One day when we were with Corrie's favourite cousin, with whom she had spent many childhood days, in an intimate restaurant in Amsterdam, she said to Corrie: "Your mother was beautifully slim." Was "beautifully slim" a substitute for "too thin" as a consequence of Bep's thyroid problem? At the time, we did not know what to make of the information, and later on we never asked the cousin precisely what she meant. In the first years after the war, relatives were afraid of opening wounds; whenever there were veiled references to an event, they never discussed it further.

In sharp contrast to this attitude was what happened on our wedding day, 2 April 1955. It was a beautiful day, and a great number of relatives, friends, and acquaintances came to City Hall, a trip that required slightly more planning than usual because of a strike of municipal transportation and utility workers. These minor obstacles did not dampen our spirits, and even the rather drab atmosphere at City Hall did not affect the cheerful mood. Neither of us being religious, we had opted solely for a civil wedding. The officiating clerk, representative of the municipality of Amsterdam, was nondescript but not unfriendly. He followed the rules of the standard protocol, declaring that so and so appeared before him in order to be joined in matrimony...stating my name and date of birth, son of (my parents' names and dates of birth were read out), after which he looked up, made eye contact with my parents, and concluded, "Here present." After the groom, it was the bride's turn. When the clerk read out the names and birth dates of

Corrie's parents, I had the impression that the audience froze and I did not want him to continue. However, without changing his monotonous drone he went on: "Both deceased, most likely in or near Auschwitz-Birkenau during the period of 24-27 October 1944."

It was not easy for the survivors to talk about Flip and Bep. Uncle Piet and his family had stayed in Theresienstadt until the Liberation by the Russians, and Cor and Lion and their seven children had been sent to Switzerland in the winter of 1944-45 in one of the rare exchanges the Red Cross managed to organize. They spent the last months of the war near the shores of Lake Geneva, in what seemed incredible luxury. In the course of the years after our wedding, a few more isolated glimpses of life in the camp were offered to us, but these raised as many questions as they answered.

The fact that before being deported to Auschwitz, Corrie's parents had exchanged some clothes for overalls for Bep seemed to indicate that they believed that they were being sent to a labour camp. Did they really believe it? Flip, being an inveterate optimist, possibly did, and we hoped it was true. Uncle Piet told us that his daughter Ied was the last to have seen Corrie's parents; she had been one of the few Jewish persons who were allowed to be near the train. She had even helped to carry their luggage. However, it was an episode in her life she found extremely difficult to talk about, let alone cope with.

Many years later, in 1986, after both her parents had died, Ied came to visit us in Toronto. It was one of those typical hot summer days, and we were sitting in the shade in a small park close to our house, watching our little grandson playing nearby. As often happened, our conversation drifted towards the war years, and we dwelled for a moment on the contrast between those days and the sunny present. All of a sudden Ied asked Corrie: "Do you know that I was the last to see your parents?" After our affirmative answer, she went on:

> I had been given the task of ticking off the names of the people who boarded the train. I was posted at the entrance to the platform and behind me there was a curtain. Four weeks before, when your parents were put on the list for the first time, I hid them behind the curtain. I offered to do the same once more, but they declined. Your mother was

exhausted and nervous, and maybe the thought that the Germans might take two other people in their place also played a role. It was the last big transport to leave Theresienstadt for Auschwitz.

Five years later, in the summer of 1991, we were in Prague for a colloquium on functional linguistics. After it was over, we stayed on in Prague for a few days, and we decided to visit Terezín, to pay homage to the memory of Corrie's parents. Terezín itself is a small garrison town, built during Empress Maria Theresa's reign, and still very much as it was in the eighteenth century, complete with moat and bridges. On the other side of the highway that leads from Prague to Dresden, one finds the penal camp, with huts full of impossibly narrow bunk beds, cells for solitary confinement, instruments of torture, a lounge for the SS, and an execution site. There was an impressive, well-tended cemetery outside the entrance gate, next to which a small information booth and a coffee shop discreetly reminded the visitors of the fact that the camp had become a museum, if not a tourist spot. Walking around in the camp, where the great majority of the Jewish victims of the Germans never set foot—only those who did not follow the rules were sent there—we felt like intruders, and left without having seen even half of the sights.

We crossed the highway and entered the town itself, where Corrie's parents had spent the last months of their lives. We wandered aimlessly through the streets of what had become again a Czech garrison town. Everything looked rundown and inhospitable. There was no trace of a railway station or of the curtain behind which Flip and Bep might have been hidden.

Appendix

1 / Calendar of Decrees and Actions

10 May 1940	the Germans attack the Netherlands
14 May 1940	air raid destroys centre of Rotterdam; more than 3,000 casualties; Germans threaten that the same fate will befall Utrecht, The Hague and Amsterdam
15 May 1940	capitulation, except for province of Zeeland
18 May 1940	Zeeland surrenders
1 July 1940	Jews no longer allowed to be members of the civilian air raid watch (Luchtbeschermingsdienst)
16 July 1940	law against ritual slaughtering
Summer 1940	German Jews no longer permitted to live in The Hague and coastal areas
18 October 1940	declaration of proof of Aryan race required from all civil servants, including elementary and high school teachers, professors, and researchers at universities
4 November 1940	all civil servants who are Jewish are dismissed; special arrangements concerning their salaries:

	breadwinners	others
first 3 months	85%	75%
next 5 years	70%	60%
following 5 years	60%	50%
afterwards	50%	40%

25, 26 November 1940	students from Leiden University and Delft Technical School go on strike in sympathy with the Jews; the Germans close both institutions of higher learning

End of 1940	many coffee shops, restaurants, etc., post signs that Jews are not welcome (see April 1941)
10 January 1941	compulsory registration of all fully or partly Jewish people
16 January 1941	date before which Jews have to hand in all radios
11 February 1941	provocation by Dutch Nazi police (WA *weerafdelingen* defense units) in Jewish quarter of Amsterdam; WA man Hendrik Koot dies
12 February 1941	Jewish quarter closed, cut off from rest of city
12, 13 February 1941	creation of Jewish Council (*Joodse Raad*) after the Eastern European model
18 February 1941	Jews to be removed from the lists of blood donors for the Red Cross before 1 March 1941
19 February 1941	Ernst Cahn, owner of an ice cream parlour in the southern part of Amsterdam, arrested after Nazi invaders who wanted to ransack his parlour are sprayed with acid (Cahn is executed on 3 March 1941, after torture and interrogation during which he does not reveal his accomplices; he is the very first victim to die by firing squad in the Netherlands)
22, 23 February 1941	about 425 Jewish "hostages" rounded up in the centre of Amsterdam and sent to Mauthausen via Schoorl and Buchenwald; (except for three, the only survivors, who were not sent to Mauthausen)
25, 26 February 1941	general strike out of solidarity with the Jews, staged in Amsterdam and a few surrounding municipalities
28 February 1941	Jewish associations and foundations registered and put under supervision
12 March 1941	Jewish businesses and enterprises put under trusteeship (German: *Verwaltung*)
End of March 1941	Haarlem (with its fiercely Nazi mayor) announces that hotels, restaurants, cafés, theatres, movie houses, public libraries, swimming pools, and bathhouses are out of bounds for Jews (Dutch: *Voor Joden verboden*)

Appendix

April 1941	Haarlem's rules apply in the whole country
11 April 1941	first issue of the *Jewish Weekly*, in which all German decrees will be published; the non-Jewish press does not publish them so that the Dutch people do not know what is going on
April 1941	orchestras dismiss Jewish musicians
21 August 1941	Jewish students banned from public schools in Amsterdam, Rotterdam, and The Hague, starting 1 September; elsewhere the deadline is 1 October
September 1941	all Jewish libraries, among them some with world-renowned collections of Judaica, closed and sealed; much of contents shipped to Germany
15 September 1941	membership in dancing schools, bridge clubs, tennis clubs, etc., no longer permitted for Jews
26 November 1941	German Jews not residing in Germany lose their German citizenship; all their holdings are confiscated
5 December 1941	all non-Dutch Jews ordered to register for "voluntary" emigration
End of the year 1941	identity card compulsory for everyone over 15 years of age; Jews get a "J" stamped on card, people with two Jewish grandparents a "BI" (Bastard I), and people with one Jewish grandparent a "BII" (Bastard II)
10 January 1942	first contingent of Jewish men (1,402) sent to labour camps in the northeast of the country, mainly in the province of Drenthe (see 1 October, 1942)
March 1942	Jews can no longer use private cars; for funerals exemption is given for the corpses; ambulances are also exempted
25 March 1942	it is forbidden to marry a non-Jewish partner; Jewish partners in mixed couples who announce a marriage at a city hall (many such marriages were planned, or had recently taken place, in order to save the Jewish half of the couple) are arrested and eventually sent to their deaths in Poland or Germany

May 1942	Jews are not allowed to shop in stores where meat, fish, and vegetables are sold
June 1942	the stores still open to Jews can only be visited from 3 p.m. until 5 p.m.; all home delivery is forbidden
End of June 1942	a) long list of professions forbidden for Jews made public b) ban against Jewish access to private establishments such as health resorts, or to the private homes of non-Jews c) special curfew for Jews from 8 p.m. to 6 a.m. d) Jews banned from public transport
End of June 1942	first decree summoning Jews between the ages of 16 and 32 to register and show up for work in Germany and Poland
15 July 1942	the first train with more than a thousand people in boxcars leaves for Auschwitz from Westerbork, Drenthe
20 July 1942	Jews no longer allowed to own or use bicycles; some exemptions are listed; these are later cancelled
1 October 1942	all inmates of labour camps in the east of the Netherlands are deported to Auschwitz via Westerbork; all relatives who stayed behind are to follow before Christmas 1942; total: about 8,000 inmates and 22,000 relatives
End of December 1942	first residents arrive at the special camp for Jews in Barneveld
15 January 1943	all foundlings of whatever origin to be considered Jewish
22, 23 January 1943	evacuation of the Jewish psychiatric hospital, Het Apeldoornse Bos; all patients and many members of the medical and support staff are *abgeschoben* deported to Auschwitz; the patients are gassed upon arrival, 25 January 1943
February 1943	the coastal communities of Haarlem, Bloemendaal, Voorschoten, and Heemstede are closed to Jews

Appendix

1 April 1943	non-Jewish civil servants married to Jewish partners are fired
10 April 1943	no Jews allowed in the following provinces: Groningen, Friesland, Drenthe, Overyssel, Gelderland, Noordbrabant, Limburg, and Zeeland
23 April 1943	no Jews allowed in the provinces of Utrecht, Zuidholland, and Noordholland, except Amsterdam
29 April 1943	sterilization rules published for Jewish partners of mixed marriages; presented as "free choice," the alternative being deportation to Poland
23 May 1943	no Jews allowed in Amsterdam
26 May 1943	first large-scale raid to round up all Jews without a special permit who live in the centre of Amsterdam
20 June 1943	second large-scale raid in the southern and eastern parts of the city
29 September 1943	the last members of the Jewish Council still remaining in Amsterdam, together with other prominent members of the Jewish community who had special permits, deported to Westerbork; all Jews staying in Barneveld are also deported to Westerbork
2 February 1944	the Portuguese Jewish community, numbering about 4,500 in 1941 of whom 4,250 live in Amsterdam, loses its special status; all sent to Auschwitz via Westerbork and Theresienstadt
14 March 1944	the last remaining patients (70) in the Joodse Invalide, a combination of hospital and nursing home, are deported; the building in the centre of Amsterdam is confiscated
3 September 1944	the last train leaves from Westerbork to Auschwitz
27 January 1945	Auschwitz liberated by the Russians
12 April 1945	Westerbork liberated by the Canadians
23 April 1945	many inmates of Bergen-Belsen are evacuated in cattle trains that carry them aimlessly through Germany

	without food or water; liberated by the Russians, near Troebitz after 14 days
5 May 1945	the Germans in the Netherlands surrender unconditionally
7, 9 May 1945	the Russians liberate Theresienstadt

2 / Concentration Camps in the Netherlands

Exclusively for Jews
1 / transit camp Westerbork (100,000 people passed through it; at the end of the war, the Canadians liberated 865 inmates)
2 / elite camp Barneveld (fewer than 700 people, most of whom survived)
3 / camp Doetinchem for Nazi sympathizers (very small, perhaps holding 25 people)
4 / training school for Dutch SS, Ellecom, where about 180 Jews were used as "training material"

All but Westerbork were closed long before the end of the war

Other camps where Jews were temporarily held, often receiving much harsher treatment than non-Jewish inmates
1 / Vught, with an almost permanent, strictly separate Jewish section
2 / Amersfoort, mainly for non-Jews; Jews were sent there as a punishment
3 / Ommen, a smaller camp also used as a transit point for non-Jews who were sent from there to factories in Germany; among others, in May 1943, the students who had refused to sign the declaration of loyalty to the German authorities, but who had not gone into hiding
4 / Schoorl, a small camp; the only Jews who were there, for a short period, were those rounded up in February 1941

3 / Numbers

When the Germans invaded the Netherlands, about 140,000 Jews lived there, 80,000 of them in Amsterdam. At Liberation, only 24,000 were alive in the whole country, including Amsterdam, and in Amsterdam itself, 14,500.

Appendix

Of the 107,000 Jews deported, fewer than 6,000 returned; 98 trains left the Netherlands, 93 of them from Westerbork.

Most deportees were sent to Auschwitz (more than 60,000, of whom 1,000 survived), and to Sobibor (34,000, with only 19 survivors).

After 2 November 1944, no more gassings took place in Auschwitz, after an order came from Berlin to stop this practice.

Of the 33,000 Jews who were not deported, 14,000 were in mixed marriages or succeeded in having their status as Jews changed; 3,000 managed to escape to safety, mainly via Belgium and France to Switzerland or Spain; 24,000 went into hiding, but of these only 16,000 survived; the others were caught by the Germans or Dutch Nazi police, some after having been denounced by fellow Dutch citizens.

In Memoriam, published by Sdu Uitgeverij, Koninginnegracht, The Hague, 1995, contains the names of more than 100,000 victims, with place and date of death. Among them are the names of my friends and family:

Alexander Rimini	Auschwitz	30.09.1942
Thérèse Duijts	Auschwitz	30.09.1942
Freddie Rozenberg	Auschwitz	25.01.1943
Johan Leonard Jacobs	Auschwitz	19.11.1943
Salomon Philip Frenkel	Auschwitz	24.10.1944
Betsy Adèle Frenkel-Wiener	Auschwitz	24.10.1944

Books in the Life Writing Series Published by Wilfrid Laurier University Press

Haven't Any News: Ruby's Letters from the Fifties
edited by Edna Staebler with an Afterword by Marlene Kadar
1995 / x + 165 pp. / ISBN 0-88920-248-6

"I Want to Join Your Club": Letters from Rural Children, 1900-1920
edited by Norah L. Lewis with a Preface by Neil Sutherland
1996 / xii + 250 pp. (30 b&w photos) / ISBN 0-88920-260-5

And Peace Never Came by Elisabeth M. Raab with Historical Notes by Marlene Kadar
1996 / x + 196 pp. (12 b&w photos, map) / ISBN 0-88920-281-8

Dear Editor and Friends: Letters from Rural Women of the North-West, 1900-1920
edited by Norah L. Lewis
1998 / xvi + 166 pp. (20 b&w photos) / ISBN 0-88920-287-7

The Surprise of My Life: An Autobiography by Claire Drainie Taylor
with a Foreword by Marlene Kadar
1998 / xii + 268 pp. (+ 8 colour photos and 92 b&w photos) / ISBN 0-88920-302-4

Memoirs from Away: A New Found Land Girlhood by Helen M. Buss / Margaret Clarke
1998 / xvi + 153 pp. / ISBN 0-88920-350-4

The Life and Letters of Annie Leake Tuttle: Working for the Best
by Marilyn Färdig Whiteley
1999 / xviii + 150 pp. / ISBN 0-88920-330-X

Marian Engel's Notebooks: "Ah, mon cahier, écoute" edited by Christl Verduyn
1999 / viii + 576 pp. / ISBN 0-88920-333-4 cloth / ISBN 0-88920-349-0 paper

Be Good Sweet Maid: The Trials of Dorothy Joudrie by Audrey Andrews
1999 / vi + 276 pp. / ISBN 0-88920-334-2

Working in Women's Archives: Researching Women's Private Literature and Archival Documents edited by Helen M. Buss and Marlene Kadar
2001 / vi + 120 pp. / ISBN 0-88920-341-5

Repossessing the World: Reading Memoirs by Contemporary Women
by Helen M. Buss
2002 / xxvi + 206 pp. / ISBN 0-88920-408-X cloth / ISBN 0-88920-410-1 paper

Chasing the Comet: A Scottish-Canadian Life by Patricia Koretchuk
2002 / xx + 244 pp. / ISBN 0-88920-407-1

The Queen of Peace Room by Magie Dominic
2002 / xii + 115 pp. / ISBN 0-88920-417-9

China Diary: The Life of Mary Austin Endicott by Shirley Jane Endicott
2002 / xvi + 251 pp. / ISBN 0-88920-412-8

The Curtain: Witness and Memory in Wartime Holland by Henry G. Schogt
2003 / xii + 132 pp. / ISBN 0-88920-396-2

www.ingramcontent.com/pod-product-compliance
Lightning Source LLC
Chambersburg PA
CBHW030445300426
44112CB00009B/1166